POSTCARDS FROM
GREECE

Recipes from across the Greek seas

REBECCA SEAL

PHOTOGRAPHY BY STEVEN JOYCE

hardie grant books

For Elodie and Rosa

Introduction

Each Greek island has its own unique culture and personality, but the same thread runs between them all: a deep, deep love for good food. There are many hundreds of islands scattered around the coast of Greece, set in glittering turquoise waters. Some are little more than rocky outcrops buffeted by waves, others are home to just a few houses and a brilliant white church perched on the sea's edge, while still others are bigger, with their own mountain ranges and craggy, sun-baked interiors. Regardless of their physical differences, on every island food is always taken seriously. It could be silvery fresh fish, just landed and turned into a seaside lunch, slow-cooked mountain goat, stewed overnight in a wood oven's cooling embers, a crisp salad laced with sharp capers or tangy cheese, or sweet preserved fruits. Ask anyone, even chefs, where the best place is to eat on their island... and they will invariably say it is at their mother's kitchen table.

Each island is rightly proud of their food traditions and I was very lucky that so many people were willing to share flavours and recipes with me. There is much to discover beyond the tourist favourites. Sardines, tzatziki and cheese saganaki are all well and good, but venture off the beaten track and you'll find a wealth of delicious dishes on whichever island you choose to visit: try lamb slow-cooked with tomatoes and chickpeas as served on Rhodes, lemony *kakavia* fish stew cooked on deck by island fisherman with their smallest, un-sellable catch, tomato bread or watermelon tart from Milos, or fennel pies made with foraged greens as eaten on Crete.

This collection of recipes represents just a taste of the foods of the Greek islands; to catalogue them all would take a (very happy) lifetime.

A note on ingredients

CHEESE

Outside Greece, we are most familiar with feta cheese, the tangy, crumbly white sheeps' milk cheese that is often the only true Greek cheese stocked in our shops (halloumi is a Greek-Cypriot cheese). I have given easily available alternatives to Greek cheeses in all the recipes in this book, but should you be lucky enough to find some, here is what to look out for. *Graviera* is a hard yellow cheese, similar to gruyère; *mizithra* is either a creamy soft cheese quite like ricotta, or an aged grating cheese; *kasseri* is used a lot like mozzarella – although it is a sheeps' and sometimes goats' milk cheese – and it melts well; *kefalotiri* is a hard, fairly strong cheese, made from sheeps' and goats' milk, served by itself to nibble or grated over pasta in the same way as parmesan or pecorino; *kopanisti* is a peppery white soft cheese; while *manouri* is a creamy soft cheese with a taste similar to that of feta.

GREEK OREGANO

Oregano grown in Greece is usually of very high quality and really rich in flavour. I recommend using it over other types if possible, which is why I call for it specifically in these recipes, as it even keeps its flavour well when dried. Fresh oregano is used in Greek cooking too (it's lovely in salads or as part of an olive oil and lemon dressing for a warm potato salad), so try growing it in a pot on the windowsill, drying some of it to use over the winter.

OLIVE OIL

Delicious olive oil is abundant in Greece and is rarely expensive; in fact the Greeks consume the most olive oil per head in the world. You are never far from an olive grove and some of the country's olive trees are themselves truly ancient: one of the oldest is at Vouves on Crete and is thought to be 3,000 years old. Greek cooks almost always use olive oil for cooking as well as in dressings and sauces. Save your best extra-virgin for dishes in which it won't be cooked and use regular olive oil for frying (vegetable oil is also fine for this, but don't tell your Greek friends if you do so...).

PASTA

Don't be surprised to see several pasta recipes in this book; Greek cookery has a pasta tradition that is easily as long as that of Italy. Centuries of trading across the Mediterranean, plus periods of the occupation of Greece by peoples such as the Venetians, influenced cooks in the Greek islands, just as their own techniques were carried far afield in turn.

Teaspoons, tablespoons and cups

This book uses American cup measurements, i.e. 237 ml for 1 cup; in the UK and Australia a cup is 250 ml and British and Australian cooks (if using cups) should be scant with their cup measurements.

1 teaspoon = 5 ml
1 tablespoon = 15ml
1 cup = 237 ml

Oven temperatures

It is important to note that I use a fan oven. If you use a conventional oven you may need to increase your temperatures by 10°C.

BREADS & PASTRIES

TINY PIES, FILLED WITH
FORAGED GREENS OR LOCAL
CHEESES, ARE COOKED
ALL OVER THE ISLANDS OF
GREECE (AS WELL AS THE
MAINLAND), AND HAVE
BEEN FOR CENTURIES. THEY
WOULD HAVE BEEN MADE
IN THE EARLY MORNINGS
AND HANDED OUT TO THOSE
LEAVING HOME TO WORK
IN THE FIELDS, ON BOATS,
OR AS SHEEP AND GOAT
HERDERS. NOW, THEY MAKE
WONDERFUL MEZEDES OR
SNACKS, AS DO LADENIA –
FLUFFY, DOUGHY TOMATO-
TOPPED BREADS FROM THE
ISLAND OF MILOS.

LAÐENIA

This recipe is based on one given to me by the wonderful Vasiliki Drounga, the owner of Paleos cafe and pastry shop in Plaka, a beautiful hilltop town on Milos. *Ladenia* are also known as Milos pizzas, so you could easily experiment with other toppings. Vasiliki explained that some people add olives to their *ladenia*, but in such a way as to suggest she thought those people were wrong…

It works best to cook these in 20 cm (8 in) lipped round trays with fixed bases, but you can also treat them like pizzas and shape the dough into rounds yourself. However, if you do so, cook them on a deep baking tray with raised edges, otherwise oil will drip into your oven.

MAKES 2 × 20 cm breads, enough for 4 as a main, or 8–10 as a meze or starter

TOPPING
800 g (1 lb 12 oz) ripe cherry tomatoes, halved
2 onions, sliced
1 teaspoon dried Greek oregano
leaves from 4 sprigs of thyme
6 tablespoons olive oil
salt and freshly ground black pepper

DOUGH
175 ml (6 fl oz/¾ cup) water
1 tablespoon active dry yeast
¼ teaspoon caster (superfine) sugar
1 teaspoon olive oil, plus 4 tablespoons for greasing
250 g (9 oz/2 cups) strong white (bread) flour, plus more to dust
¾ teaspoon fine salt

Preheat the oven to 200°C (400°F/Gas 6).

Start with the topping. Toss together the cherry tomatoes, onions, Greek oregano, thyme and 4 tablespoons of the olive oil. Season and place in a single layer on a baking tray. Cook in the oven for 15–20 minutes, until the onions are golden and the tomatoes are beginning to brown and soften.

Make the dough: mix the water, yeast and sugar together in a jug and leave to stand for 10 minutes; the yeast will get to work and the liquid will develop a foamy head. Whisk in the 1 teaspoon of olive oil.

Put the flour and salt in a large mixing bowl, add the yeast mixture and mix thoroughly; the dough will be fairly sticky at this stage. On a floured surface, start to knead the dough, using floured hands and knuckles to stretch the dough out before folding it back on itself. (If it is really too sticky to do this, add a tablespoon or two more flour to the mix.) Knead for 10 minutes, by which time the dough will be smooth and pliable. Place the dough in an oiled bowl, cover and leave in a warm place for about an hour or until doubled in size. (Depending on the temperature, it may take longer to double in size. You can tell when it has finished rising as the dough will dent rather than spring back when you press it.)

Once the dough has risen, knock it back: use your hands to squash it back to roughly its original size.

Oil two 20 cm (8 in) round baking trays with 2 tablespoons of olive oil, or oil one large baking tray with 4 tablespoons of oil. Divide the dough into two. Stretch and push each piece out either to fill a 20 cm (8 in) round baking tray, or to form one of two 20 cm (8 in) circles for the large baking tray. Using your fingertips, gently dimple the surface of the dough. Set aside for 15 minutes to rise again.

Preheat the oven to 200°C (400°F/Gas 6) once more.

When ready to cook, divide the tomato and onion evenly over the bases. Drizzle 1 tablespoon of olive oil over each and place them in the oven. Cook for 20 minutes, until the dough has puffed up and is golden brown and the tomatoes are completely cooked. Eat while still warm.

SFAKIAN CHEESE PIES WITH HONEY

Little pies, called *pita*, stuffed with cheese, vegetables or meat, are popular all over the country and have a culinary history stretching back to the cooks of Ancient Greece. In countryside villages and on the islands, they would have been made in the morning, filled with whatever food was to hand and given to workers heading out to the fields, olive groves or the mountains to herd sheep and goats, to eat later in the day. Almost every town or village still has its own special pie, using local ingredients. This is my adaptation of a recipe from Sfakia, a village in southern Crete.

These little sweet cheese pies are served as mezedes or starters, but they are equally tasty at brunch. You can leave out the alcohol if you prefer, just replace it with the same amount of water; however it is a very traditional ingredient in many pie recipes and lends a lovely subtle flavour to the pastry.

MAKES ABOUT 10, enough for 2 for brunch, or 4–5 as a meze
2 tablespoons olive oil, plus more for frying
200 g (7 oz/1⅔ cups) plain (all-purpose) flour, plus more to dust
½ teaspoon fine salt
2 tablespoons ouzo, raki or other aniseed liquor (optional)
250 g (9 oz/1⅔ cups) mozzarella, chopped
clear honey, ideally from thyme or rosemary honey, to serve

Mix the oil, flour, salt, ouzo (if using) and enough water (up to about 4 tablespoons, or 6 if you don't use the alcohol) to make a firm dough. Knead for 5 minutes until smooth, then wrap in plastic wrap and leave to rest at room temperature for 20 minutes.

When the dough has rested, roll out on a lightly floured surface until 1–2 mm (⅛ in) thick, and, using a 7.5 cm (3 in) round cutter, or a saucer, cut out around 20 circles (you will need an even number). Wet your fingertip and run a little water around the edge of each. Divide the mozzarella evenly between half of the circles and top each with the remaining circles. Press down lightly to seal; the pies should be fairly flat.

Warm 1 tablespoon of oil in a wide frying pan and fry the pies until golden brown on both sides. Fry in batches, so as not to crowd the pan, and keep the cooked pies warm while you cook the rest, adding more oil as necessary, bringing it up to temperature before adding the next batch of pies. Serve warm, drizzled with honey.

WILD GREENS PIES

On Crete these are called *marathopites*, and they're similar to a pie I have eaten on Rhodes, called *pougia* (which may also be made with cheese or sweet fillings). Feel free to play around with the flavourings here. Grated fennel is very traditional, finely chopped wild garlic or herbs such as sorrel are wonderful additions, or try a little feta. The pies are a classic example of the ingenuity of island cooks: the herbs and greens are often foraged from the islands' stunning mountainous interiors. Living in a city I've used spinach instead.

MAKES 16, enough for 6–8 as a meze or starter

DOUGH
2 tablespoons olive oil, plus more for frying
200 g (7 oz/1⅔ cups) plain (all-purpose) flour, plus more to dust
½ teaspoon fine salt
2 tablespoons ouzo, raki or other aniseed liquor (optional)

FILLING
60–70 g (2–2¼ oz/1 packed cup) spinach leaves, finely chopped
2 tablespoons parsley leaves, finely chopped
3 spring onions (scallions), finely chopped
1 tablespoon dill (dillweed), finely chopped
1 garlic clove, grated
salt and freshly ground black pepper
1–2 tablespoons lemon juice

First, make the dough. Mix the oil, flour, salt, ouzo (if using) and enough water (up to about 4 tablespoons, or 6 if you don't use the alcohol) to make a firm dough. Knead for five minutes until smooth, then wrap in plastic wrap and leave to rest at room temperature for 20 minutes.

Mix together the filling and season with salt, pepper and lemon juice.

Roll out the pastry on a lightly floured surface until it is 2 mm (⅛ in) thick. Using a knife, cut rectangles measuring roughly 8 × 6 cm (3¼ × 2½ in). Place a small spoonful of the filling into the centre of each rectangle, then fold the corners over the filling, like an envelope, to encase it. Wet your fingers and seal the edges firmly. Set aside while you make the rest.

Heat about 1 cm (½ in) of olive oil in a wide pan and gently fry the parcels in batches for a couple of minutes on each side, taking care not to crowd the pan, until covered in golden brown speckles. Keep the cooked pies warm while you cook the rest, adding more oil as necessary, bringing it up to temperature before adding the next batch of pies. Eat straightaway, while warm.

CHEESE PIES FROM ALONISSOS

I first tried – far too many – of these dangerously tasty goats' cheese pies on one of my earliest trips to Greece, just after I finished university. I remember packing a little picnic of a few of them and some watermelon and hiring a boat down the coast to an inaccessible and deserted beach with black sand.

There is a little friendly rivalry between the residents of Alonissos, a small and relatively unspoiled island in the Sporades group islands, and those of neighbouring Skopelos, as both believe they invented these delicacies.

MAKES 10, enough for 10 as a meze or starter
350 g (12 oz/3 cups) soft, mild rindless goats' cheese
10 sheets of filo pastry, each measuring about 20 cm (8 in) square
flavourless vegetable oil and olive oil for frying

Keep the remaining filo covered with a damp tea towel while you make each pie, as filo dries out and becomes brittle very fast.

Lay a pastry square out on a work surface. Scatter 35 g (1¼ oz) of the cheese over the pastry, avoiding the left and right hand edges by about 4 cm (1¾ in) on each side. Working from the furthest edge of the pastry, turn the pastry down over the cheese, so it covers half the remaining pastry. Do the same with the bottom edge, so the cheese is completely covered. Pinch together both the right- and left-hand edges of the pastry and pull one end round to coil it into a spiral; be gentle or the pastry will rip.

Pour about 5 mm (¼ in) each of the vegetable and olive oils into a wide pan with high sides placed over a high heat. When it is hot, reduce the heat to medium.

Using a wide spatula, slide the pastry spirals into the hot oil, in batches, being sure not to crowd the pan. If it looks as though any of them might unravel, place the loose end of the spiral against the edge of the frying pan; as soon as it starts to crisp up it will hold its shape. Fry for about 4 minutes or until the pastry is golden brown on the bottom. Using the spatula and a wooden spoon, very carefully flip the cheese pies over, being sure not to splash yourself with hot oil. Fry the other sides until golden brown all over and crisp on the edges. Remove from the hot oil and drain on paper towels. Keep warm while you cook the remaining pastries, adding more oil if necessary, bringing it up to temperature before adding the next batch of pies. Serve while hot.

CHEESE & ONION PIES

These little half moon-shaped pies, *pitarakia*, are from Milos. Vinegar may seem like an odd addition to pastry, but it really does work. I found a similar recipe in a book, *The Best Traditional Recipes of Milos Island*, a collection of lovely old hand-me-down specialities, kindly given to me by the daughter of the author, Chrissoula Vihou. She and the mayor of Milos sent me on my way with a huge basket of Milos delicacies: dried tomatoes, *pasteli* sesame sweets (page 228), spoon sweets (page 210), local honey, preserves and hand-made pasta, from the shop, Paradossiakia Edesmata, in Adamas, which every food lover who goes to Milos must visit.

MAKES 20, enough for 4–8 as a meze

DOUGH
200 g (7 oz/1⅔ cups) plain (all-purpose) flour, plus more to dust
1 tablespoon olive oil, plus more for frying
1 teaspoon white wine vinegar
½ teaspoon fine salt
about 100 ml (3½ fl oz/scant ½ cup) water

FILLING
40 g (1½ oz/⅓ cup) grated pecorino romano
160 g (5¾ oz/1¼ cups) grated gruyère
4 shallots, grated

Mix the flour, oil, vinegar and salt together in a large bowl, then gradually add the water, mixing with your hands. Stop adding water when the dough is firm; don't allow it to become sticky. (Add a little more flour if you accidentally add too much water.) Knead it for 2 or 3 minutes until the dough is smooth. Set aside to rest for 30 minutes. Meanwhile, mix all the filling ingredients together.

On a floured work surface, roll the pastry out until it is 2 mm (⅛ in) thick (you may need to do this in batches unless you have a very big counter). Using a round 10 cm (4 in) cutter (or a saucer), cut out circles of the pastry. You should be able to make 20 if you collect up and re-roll the trimmings. Wet your finger and run it round the edges of each circle. Then, place a heaped spoonful of filling on one side of each. Fold the pastry over the cheese to form a semi-circle. Press the wet edges together with the tines of a fork.

Warm about 5 mm (¼ in) of olive oil in a wide frying pan over a medium heat. Working in batches, fry the pitarakia in the oil for 1–2 minutes a side until golden and the pastry has bubbled slightly. Keep warm while you cook the remaining pastries, adding more oil if necessary, bringing it up to temperature before adding the next batch. Eat while hot.

KESSARIA PIES

These are indulgent little pies, filled with béchamel and crisp pancetta, that I discovered on Kos. Avoid cooking with filo that has been caked in cornflour in the package, as it can give a mealy, gritty feel in the mouth when cooked.

MAKES ABOUT 15, enough for 6–8 as a meze or starter
125 g (4 oz/1 stick) butter
2 tablespoons plain (all-purpose) flour
300 ml (½ pint/1¼ cups) hot milk
freshly ground black pepper
20 g (¾ oz/scant ¼ cup) grated pecorino
150 g (5 oz/⅔ cup) pancetta, cubed
5 long sheets of filo pastry, around 200 g (7 oz) in total

Preheat the oven to 180°C (350°F/Gas 4).

Melt 25 g (1 oz/2 tablespoons) of the butter in a pan over a gentle heat. Add the flour and cook, stirring, for 3 or 4 minutes. Gradually add the hot milk, but don't go too fast or the sauce will become lumpy. Once you have a smooth béchamel sauce, add a little black pepper and the pecorino. Cook for a couple of minutes longer, stirring often, then remove from the heat and set aside.

Sauté the pancetta in a dry pan over a medium heat until crisp. Stir it into the béchamel. Set aside and allow to cool: the cooler the béchamel, the easier it is to work with.

Melt the remaining butter and cool slightly. Use a little to liberally grease a large baking tray.

Keep any filo you are not working with covered with a damp tea towel, as it can dry out and become brittle very quickly. Lay the first sheet of pastry on a work surface. The varying size and shape of ready-made filo pastry may mean you will have to trim it, or you can make smaller or larger pastry tubes. Make a rectangle roughly 20 × 15 cm (8 × 6 in) and brush it with butter. Working across one of the shorter ends, spread 1 tablespoonful of the béchamel in a line, keeping it about 3 cm (1¼ in) from the edges. Fold the short edge over the béchamel by about 3 cm (1¼ in). Turn the long sides in by about 1 cm (½ in), over the filled section of pastry and all the way down the sides. Leave plenty of room between the fold and the beginning of the filling as the filling will expand in the oven and without the extra space the tube of pastry may burst. Brush with butter all the along the newly exposed pastry edges. Gently turn the filled end of the pastry over once to begin to create a roll. Brush the newly exposed pastry with butter. Repeat for four turns in total, brushing with butter each time. Trim off any excess pastry.

Place the roll on the prepared baking sheet and brush with butter, ensuring all the exposed pastry has butter on it. Repeat until all the filling has been used up.

Place the tray in the oven and bake for 12–15 minutes, or until golden brown and crisp all over. Serve warm.

FLATBREADS

On many of the islands, pita (or pitta) bread – the bread we associate most with Greece – isn't eaten that frequently, instead, rusks (page 61) or wholemeal loaves are more popular. However, you can't make souvlaki (page 153) without good flatbreads, plus these are great lightly toasted and cut into strips, ready to scoop up any number of delicious Greek dips and meze.

MAKES 8 breads
350 ml (12 fl oz/1½ cups) lukewarm water
1 tablespoon active dry yeast
1 tablespoon caster (superfine) sugar
2 tablespoons olive oil, plus more for the bowl and for frying
500 g (1 lb 2 oz/4 cups) strong white (bread) flour, plus more to dust
2 teaspoons fine salt

Mix the water, yeast, sugar and oil together in a jug and leave to stand for 10 minutes. The yeast will get to work and the liquid will develop a foamy head.

Put the flour and salt in a large mixing bowl, add the yeast mixture and mix thoroughly. The dough will be fairly sticky at this stage. On a floured surface, start to knead the dough, using floured hands and knuckles to stretch the dough out, before folding it back on itself. (If it is really too sticky to do this, add a tablespoon or two of flour to the mix.) Knead for 10 minutes, by which time the dough will be smooth and pliable. Place the dough in an oiled bowl, cover and leave in a warm place for about an hour, or until doubled in size. (Depending on the temperature, it may take longer to double in size. You can tell when it has finished rising as the dough will dent rather than spring back when you press it.)

Once the dough has risen, knock it back: use your hands to squash it back to roughly its original size.

Divide into 8 equal balls. Dust a work surface and rolling pin with flour and roll out until 5 mm (¼ in) thick and about 20 cm (8 in) in diameter. Using a fork, gently prick the breads all over, being careful not to poke all the way through the dough. Set aside for 10 minutes.

Get a wide frying pan hot over a medium-heat. Have ready a clean tea towel. Pour a splash of olive oil on a sheet of paper towel and wipe around the pan. Place the first bread into the pan and cook for 2–3 minutes, until golden brown bubbles and flecks appear on the bottom. Flip and cook for 2 more minutes, pressing down gently if the bread puffs up. Remove from the pan when golden brown bubbles have appeared on that side too, and wrap in the tea towel to steam and keep warm until the other breads are ready.

Wipe the pan with the oiled sheet of paper towel again, and cook the rest of the breads in the same way.

In the quiet early mornings, before the islands come to life, the light on the water is breathtaking.

MEZEDES & SALADS

THERE IS LITTLE BETTER IN LIFE THAN A SUNNY AFTERNOON – PREFERABLY BY THE SEA – LINGERING OVER A FEW LITTLE MEZE DISHES WITH A GLASS OF CHILLED WINE. THERE ARE HUNDREDS OF DISHES SERVED ACROSS THE ISLANDS TO CHOOSE BETWEEN – FROM DELICIOUS TZATZIKI, SERVED EVERYWHERE, TO MORE UNUSUAL DISHES, LIKE DELICATE CHICKPEA FRITTERS; CRUNCHY DAKOS TOPPED WITH FRESH TOMATO, OREGANO AND FETA; OR TIROKAFTERI, A SPICY CHEESE DIP.

TOMATO FRITTERS FROM SANTORINI

These tangy fritters, *domatokeftedes*, made from both fresh and dried tomatoes, make a lovely meze. Be sure to buy good-quality sun-dried tomatoes, as some mass-produced versions can have a mushy texture and a muddy flavour. On the island of Milos, cooks make a similar dish with chopped garlic added to the batter, while on other islands they add hard *kefalotyri* cheese. As long as your sun-dried tomatoes are not too salty, you can experiment with feta or pecorino.

MAKES 20
100 g (3½ oz/⅔ cup) sun-dried tomatoes, dried or preserved in oil
400 g (14 oz) tomatoes
3 spring onions (scallions), finely chopped
1 tablespoon finely chopped parsley leaves, plus more to serve
1 tablespoon finely chopped mint leaves
generous pinch of dried Greek oregano
¼ teaspoon baking powder
80–90 g (3¼ oz/¾ cup) plain (all-purpose) flour
vegetable or olive oil for frying
salt, to taste, if needed

If using dry tomatoes, rehydrate them in hot water for 20 minutes. If using sun-dried tomatoes in oil, drain off the oil. Deseed the fresh tomatoes, over a bowl to retain the juice. Strain off the juice and discard the seeds. Using a food processor or stick blender, briefly blitz together the juice, fresh and dried tomatoes, 2 of the spring onions, the herbs and baking powder; you don't want a purée but a chunky batter. Next, gradually mix in the flour (you may not need it all, though you may need more if your tomatoes are very juicy). The batter should be loose, but not so sloppy that it won't hold together at all.

Heat around 5 cm (2 in) of oil in a high-sided saucepan over a medium heat, until it reaches 180°C (350°F) on a pan thermometer, or a cube of day-old bread dropped into it sizzles and browns in 30 seconds. Take a small spoonful of batter and drop into the oil. Cook for a couple of minutes, then cool and taste for seasoning. Some sun-dried tomatoes are salty but, if yours are not, add salt to taste to the remaining batter.

Drop tablespoons of batter carefully into the hot oil, two or three at a time (if the pan is crowded the oil will cool and the fritters will be greasy). Cook for 3–3½ minutes, turning if necessary, until they are cooked through and golden brown. Sprinkle with parsley and the remaining spring onion to serve.

COURGETTE CRISPS

These little vegetable crisps are dangerously moreish and make a lovely accompaniment to a glass of white wine. The longer you salt and drain the courgette (zucchini), the crisper they will be when you fry them. Watch them carefully as they cook, because there is only a matter of seconds between golden brown and delicious and dark brown and bitter.

SERVES 4

½ teaspoon fine salt
1 courgette (zucchini), finely sliced into rounds
vegetable oil for frying
3–4 tablespoons plain (all-purpose) flour

Scatter the salt over the courgette slices, then place in a colander set over a bowl. Leave to drain, preferably overnight, in the fridge. When you are ready to cook, remove from the colander and pat dry very thoroughly using paper towels.

In a high-sided pan, heat 3 cm (1¼ in) of oil until it reaches 180°C (350°F) on an oil thermometer, or when a cube of day-old bread dropped into it sizzles and browns in 30 seconds.

Spoon the flour into a sandwich bag and add the courgette slices. Holding it firmly shut, shake gently to coat the slices in flour (you may need to do this in 2 batches). Shake off the excess and carefully drop them, 3–4 at a time, into the oil. Cook for 2–2½ minutes, or until golden brown all over. Use a slotted spoon to remove from the oil and drain on paper towels. Keep the cooked crisps warm while you fry the rest. Serve immediately.

FAVA DIP

This is one of Santorini's iconic dishes, and the island's chefs claim that their version is the best in Greece. It is true that yellow split peas from Santorini are particularly delicious. You can garnish this with a little finely sliced onion if you like, or a sprinkling of chopped parsley or dill.

SERVES 4
200 g (7 oz/1 cup) dried yellow split peas
60 ml (2 fl oz/¼ cup) olive oil
salt
½ onion, very finely chopped or grated, plus more to serve (optional)
juice of ½ lemon, or to taste
about 60 ml (2 fl oz/¼ cup) extra-virgin olive oil, plus more to serve

Soak the split peas in cold water overnight. Drain and rinse, then place in a non-reactive pan with 600 ml (1 pint/2½ cups) of fresh water and bring to the boil. Boil hard for 10 minutes. Skim off any scum that forms on the surface with a spoon. Reduce the heat, cover and simmer for 40 minutes, or until the peas are soft. You may need to add a little more water now and then, as the cooking time varies depending on the split peas, but don't add too much at a time. (And don't add salt as that will toughen the peas.)

Meanwhile, place the olive oil in a pan set over a low heat. Add a pinch of salt and the onion and soften it, gently and without browning, for about 10 minutes.

When the split peas are cooked, drain off any excess water, add the onions and their oil, the lemon juice and about half the extra-virgin oil. Blitz in a food processor or with a hand-held blender until you have a smooth purée. Taste and add more salt, extra-virgin olive oil or lemon juice, as necessary.

Allow to cool and taste again before serving. It may need loosening with a little water or more olive oil because it thickens as it cools. Just before serving, top with some onion (if using) and drizzle a little extra-virgin olive oil over the top. Serve as part of a meze, with flatbreads or toasted bread for scooping it up.

WARM COURGETTE & FETA WITH HERBS

On an unseasonably cold and blustery night in Kos, we found ourselves in a restaurant tucked away in an old school house, where the menu was written in exercise books. They served us this chunky dip as part of a warming meze. It is sometimes made with eggs, scrambled in at the last minute, in which case it makes a lovely brunch dish. (Just add two beaten eggs to the pan at the same time as you add the cheese and herbs and cook gently until the eggs are scrambled, then serve on buttered toast.) You can also make it a smoother dip, by chopping the courgette (zucchini) finely and mashing it lightly when cooked.

SERVES 4
2 large courgettes (zucchini)
salt and freshly ground black pepper
olive oil to cook
125 g (4 oz) feta
2 tablespoons chopped mint leaves
2 tablespoons chopped parsley leaves

Cut the courgettes into small chunks, sprinkle over a pinch of salt and some black pepper, then fry gently in a pan with a little olive oil, until soft and golden brown.

Remove from the heat, crumble in the cheese and add the herbs. Toss gently. Serve warm as part of a meze, with flatbreads or toasted bread for scooping it up.

ROASTED AUBERGINE & CAPER SALAD

This is a twist on a classic Greek salad. The smoky roasted aubergine (eggplant) and sharp capers work perfectly together. If you can get hold of some grey-coloured caper leaves (as in the photo), the salad will be even better. In Greece, even the caper leaves are preserved, rather than just the buds and berries.

Charring the aubergine (eggplant) this way results in an unmistakeable flavour, so if you can sit it directly on a flame, do so. Lining the base of your gas hob with foil (under the ring) will make it easier to clean up afterwards!

SERVES 2 as a main or 4 as a side dish

1 aubergine (eggplant)
lemon juice
100 g (3½ oz) cucumber, chopped into small chunks
200 g (7 oz/6 cups) salad leaves (I like chard, rocket (aragula),
spinach, mizuna)
1 tablespoon finely chopped red onion
handful of black olives, ideally plump purplish Kalamata or similar
6–8 small ripe tomatoes, halved
1 tablespoon capers
handful of parsley leaves, left whole
extra-virgin olive oil
salt and freshly ground black pepper
100 g (3½ oz) feta

Place the whole aubergine directly on a gas ring and cook, turning regularly, for about 15 minutes or until the skin has blackened and blistered and the aubergine is collapsing. Alternatively, place under the grill (broiler) and cook at maximum temperature, turning, until the skin is thoroughly charred all over. Set aside to cool for a few minutes. When cool enough to handle, place on a plate and cut from end to end, but not all the way through to the other side, opening the flesh out like a book. Using a spoon, carefully scoop out the flesh, leaving the black-ened, ashy skin behind. Place the flesh in a bowl and squeeze over a little lemon juice, to stop it discolouring. If necessary, chop it into bite-sized pieces.

In a large serving bowl, place the cucumber, salad leaves, onion, olives, tomatoes, capers and parsley. Drizzle over a little olive oil, season with salt and pepper and toss. To serve, crumble over the feta and add the aubergine, then toss once more, very gently.

SPICY CHEESE DIP

I love the combination of salty-sharp cheese and chilli heat in this dip, *tiro-kafteri*. This is a great served with some crudites or warm flatbreads.

SERVES 4–6
1 red (bell) pepper, roasted, seeded and skinned (page 74) or
60 g (2 oz/⅓ cup) cooked red pepper from a jar
100 g (3½ oz) feta
2 tablespoons Greek yoghurt
1 teaspoon lemon juice, or to taste
pinch of dried Greek oregano, or to taste
pinch of chilli flakes or chopped fresh red chilli, or to taste, plus more to serve
1 tablespoon extra-virgin olive oil
salt
very finely sliced onion to serve (optional)
fresh oregano leaves to serve (optional)

Blitz everything except the garnishes together in the food processor until you get a lovely salmon pink dip; it can be smooth or left a little chunky.

Taste and add more lemon, Greek oregano, salt or chilli, until just right: it should be rich, creamy and spicy.

If possible, make this in advance of serving and leave to let the flavours develop. Serve at room temperature, sprinkled with onion, fresh oregano leaves and chilli flakes, if you like.

RED PEPPERS STUFFED WITH CHEESE

Sweet roasted romano peppers stuffed with hot and melting cheese are very evocative of early evenings in Greece for me. I love to serve these at the beginning of a dinner party, with a glass of cold, crisp white wine.

SERVES 4

4 long red romano peppers
250 g (9 oz) feta, crumbled
1 tablespoon olive oil, plus more to brush
1 tablespoon lemon juice
2 heaped tablespoons Greek yoghurt
pinch of dried Greek oregano
2 tablespoons finely chopped parsley leaves
freshly ground black pepper
couple of pieces of bread

Preheat the oven to 200°C (400°F/Gas 6).

Cut the tops off the peppers (set them aside), and pull out the seeds. Rinse inside and out with cold water.

Mix all the other ingredients together, except the bread, and mash until well combined. Taste and check the seasoning. Using a teaspoon with as long a handle as possible, stuff the cheese into the peppers, pressing it right down into the bottom. Gently (without splitting the pepper), massage the cheese mix down the inside of the pepper. Stop about 2 cm (¾ in) from the top. Wipe any excess cheese off the outside.

Plug the open ends with a bit of bread to stop too much of the cheese spilling during cooking and replace the tops. Lightly oil a baking tray, then brush the peppers with oil and place on the baking tray. Bake in the oven for 20 minutes, until the pepper is soft and cooked. Discard the bread and serve while the filling is still warm and melting.

BAKED GIANT BEANS

Gigandes plaki makes a hearty vegetarian meze dish or supper. The beans become tasty and sweet as they slow-cook in the oven. You can buy gigantes beans from specialist food shops; if not use the largest butter (lima) beans you can find.

SERVES 4–6 as a meze, or 2 generously as a main

7 tablespoons olive oil
I onion, very finely chopped
4 garlic cloves
pinch of salt
I teaspoon tomato purée (paste)
400 g (14 oz/1⅔ cups) passata (sieved tomatoes) or blitzed canned tomatoes
3 tablespoons chopped parsley leaves
¼ teaspoon dried Greek oregano
¼ teaspoon thyme leaves or dried thyme
200 g (7 oz) raw *gigantes* or butter (lima) beans, soaked and boiled or
2 x 400 g (14 oz) cans, rinsed and drained
freshly ground black pepper

Preheat the oven to 180°C (350°F/Gas 4).

Get a wide pan hot over a low medium heat, add I tablespoon of the olive oil, the onion and garlic cloves, plus a pinch of salt. Cook for 10–15 minutes, stirring often, until the onion is translucent, golden brown and soft. Add the tomato purée and cook for a couple of minutes, stirring. Then add the passata or blended tomatoes and the herbs and cook for 10 minutes, allowing the tomatoes to break down (crush any lumpy bits with the back of a wooden spoon). Finally add the beans, stir and taste for seasoning.

Pour the mixture into a baking dish and add 200 ml (7 fl oz/scant I cup) of water. Place in the oven for 30 minutes. After this time, check to see if the dish looks as though it may need a little more water. Add 3–4 tablespoons if necessary and bake for another 30 minutes. Remove from the oven and leave to cool. This dish is usually served at room temperature, but it is also very good hot.

WALNUT, FENNEL & POMEGRANATE SALAD

With the crunch of fennel and walnut and little jewels of pomegranate, this salad is just as good to look at as it is to eat. Rather than feta, for this I prefer I use a firm white sheeps' milk cheese from Wales, which is reasonably similar to graviera or myzithra. You could also use a young pecorino.

SERVES 4

250 g (9 oz) bitter salad leaves: radichio, spinach, cos (romaine), watercress or rocket (aragula) all work well
handful of walnut pieces
2 spring onions (scallions), finely chopped
50 g (2 oz) fennel, finely sliced or shaved with a grater or potato peeler
2 tablespoons roughly chopped dill (dillweed)
1–2 tablespoons extra-virgin olive oil
1 teaspoon lemon juice
4 tablespoons pomegranate seeds
75 g (2½ oz) hard white sheeps' milk cheese

Place the salad leaves, walnuts, spring onions, fennel and dill in a serving bowl or on a platter.

Whisk the olive oil and lemon juice together and drizzle over the salad. Toss gently.

Scatter over the pomegranate seeds and, using a potato peeler or grater, shave thin slices of the cheese over the top. Serve immediately.

CHICKPEA FRITTERS

I find these squidgy-centred little fritters impossible to resist, and love to serve them with a dish of garlicky Tzatziki (page 73) on the side. There are dozens of variations to this recipe: you can add cumin, dried Greek oregano or mint, all natural partners to chickpeas, and you can easily leave out the cheese, but if you do you may need to add a little more salt. Some recipes even call for cutting the chickpeas (garbanzos) with mashed potatoes, so feel free to experiment. If you don't add the egg, this also works as a dip. The mixture firms up as it cools, so you will need to loosen it with olive oil or a little water before serving with toasted Flatbreads (page 32).

SERVES 4–6

400 g (14 oz/2⅔ cups) cooked chickpeas (garbanzos)
1 slice white bread, crusts removed
50 ml (2 fl oz/¼ cup) milk
3 spring onions (scallions), finely chopped
150 g (5 oz) feta
1 garlic clove, finely chopped
2 tablespoons finely chopped parsley leaves
1 tablespoon finely chopped dill
freshly ground black pepper
¼ teaspoon salt, or less, to taste
1 egg, lightly beaten
vegetable oil for deep-frying
plain (all-purpose) flour, to dust

Drain and rinse the chickpeas, then set aside.

Place the bread in a bowl and cover with the milk. Soak for 5 minutes, then remove from the milk and gently squeeze out the excess.

Put everything except the salt, egg, oil and flour in the bowl of a food processor and blitz until really smooth (you could also use a hand-held blender). Taste for seasoning and add salt as necessary (remember feta can be salty). Add the egg and then chill for 10 minutes or so to firm up, as this makes it easier to handle when frying.

When ready to cook, heat 6 cm (2½ in) vegetable oil in a high-sided pan, until it reaches 180°C (350°F), or when a cube of bread dropped into the oil sizzles and browns in 30 seconds.

Place some flour in a bowl. Flour your hands. Using a large dessert spoon, scoop a spoonful of the mixture into the flour. Shape into a ball (it will be quite loose but don't worry) and ensure the whole surface of the fritter is covered in flour. Using a clean spoon, drop the fritter carefully into the hot oil. Cook for 2–3 minutes, until deep golden brown and crunchy on the outside. Using a slotted spoon, remove from the oil and drain on paper towels. Break open the first one to ensure that it is cooked through; if not, cook for a minute longer. Only cook 2–3 fritters at a time, or the temperature of the oil will drop and the fritters will be greasy.

Serve hot, with Tzatziki.

ÐAKØS

Rusks, *paximádia*, are simply bread that has been dried in the oven so it keeps for longer. Originally they were made so that cooks didn't have to light a fire every day to make bread and use up valuable fuel, and they were often taken out to sea by sailors and fishermen. Nowadays, rusks are used as the base for *dakos*, a simple but lovely combination of ripe tomatoes, feta, olive oil and dried Greek oregano, or as rustic croûtons in salad (page 83). You will find dakos on islands all over the Aegean.

SERVES 4

2 small wholemeal bread rolls
300 g (10½ oz) ripe tomatoes, plus 1 more tomato
pinch of salt
1–2 tablespoons extra-virgin olive oil
100 g (3½ oz) myzithra or feta
pinch of dried Greek oregano
freshly ground black pepper

Preheat the oven to 110°C (225°F/Gas ¼). Split the rolls into halves and place them on a tray in the oven. Leave to dry out and crisp up for 1¼ hours.

Meanwhile, cut the tomatoes in half across their middles (reserving the single tomato). Place a sieve over a bowl and put a box cheese grater in it. Place a folded tea towel under the bowl to stop it slipping. Grate the tomatoes against the coarse side of the grater, placing the cut side against the grater and using the tomato skin to protect your fingers. Let the juice drain off the tomatoes, then lift the flesh out of the bowl and discard the skins and juice. Mix a pinch of salt with the grated tomato flesh, unless you have really ripe, full-flavoured tomatoes, and add 1 teaspoon of the olive oil. Chop the remaining whole tomato fairly finely, but so you still have some texture and stir it through the tomato mixture.

When the bread rolls are crisp and crunchy all the way through, remove from the oven and allow to cool.

Crumble the cheese roughly into largish chunks rather than tiny flakes.

To serve, top each piece of bread with a drizzle of olive oil, a couple of spoonfuls of the tomato mix and about a quarter of the cheese. Finish with a scattering of oregano, another drizzle of olive oil, and a couple of grinds of black pepper. Serve immediately.

OLIVE DIP

No spread of meze dishes is complete without a little bowl of this powerful olive dip, richly flavoured with plenty of garlic.

Try adding 1–2 tablespoons of Greek yoghurt. This results in a slightly more mellow flavour and a pale purple dip. Or bring it closer to the French dip tapenade by adding a few anchovies, parsley or 1 teaspoon of capers.

SERVES 4
100 g (3½ oz/½ cup) Kalamata olives, pitted (stones removed)
1 garlic clove
1 tablespoon extra-virgin olive oil

Mix all the ingredients together. Using a hand-held blender or food processor, blend until fairly smooth.

Serve with toasted bread, flatbreads or raw vegetables for dipping.

GREEN HERB SALAD

Everything except the cos (romaine) lettuce in this crisp and crunchy salad *maroulosalata*, is optional, so tailor it to your favourite flavours. It's great with or without the dill and fennel, which are distinctive tastes some people really don't enjoy. If you like, you can also add chicory, sorrel or other seasonal salad leaves.

SERVES 4

SALAD
3 or 4 leaves from a cos (romaine) lettuce, stems removed
handful of watercress
handful of rocket (arugula)
handful of spinach
leaves from 1 sprig of mint
¼ fennel bulb, very finely chopped
1 spring onion (scallion), very finely chopped
1 tablespoon very finely chopped dill (dillweed)

DRESSING
2 tablespoons extra-virgin olive oil
1 teaspoon cider vinegar
½ teaspoon lemon juice
salt and freshly ground black pepper

Wash all the leaves (including the mint) together and dry them in a salad spinner. Tip out on to a board and chop them into small slices. Add the fennel, spring onion and dill.

Whisk together the dressing ingredients and season well. Pour half of it over the salad and toss thoroughly. Add more of the dressing if needed; the salad shouldn't be oily. Serve immediately.

BEETROOT SALAD

If you can't find beetroot with leaves, use a few leaves of rainbow chard instead. This is often served with lots of pungent raw garlic. It is delicious done the traditional way, but you can skip the garlic if you prefer.

SERVES 4
400 g (14 oz) raw beetroot, with tops, in a variety of colours if possible
½–1 teaspoon lemon juice
1 teaspoon–1 tablespoon extra-virgin olive oil
salt and freshly ground black pepper
1 garlic clove, finely chopped (optional)
roughly chopped parsley leaves to serve

Preheat the oven to 200°C (400°F/Gas 6).

Gently wash off any dirt from the beetroot and their tops. Trim the tops and reserve. Wrap the beetroot in foil and place in the oven for 1 hour or until tender to the point of a knife.

Chop the beetroot tops into small pieces. Place in a pan with a little water, just 1–2 tablespoons, and cook until just wilted and soft.

Remove the beetroots from the foil and allow to cool. When cool enough to touch, rub off the skins with your thumbs. Slice and place in a mixing bowl.

Drain the beetroot tops and add to the mixing bowl. Dress with a little lemon juice, olive oil, salt and pepper. Add the garlic now too (if using). Toss everything together, then transfer to a clean serving bowl. Scatter over the parsley before serving.

SOUR CREAM & FENNEL SEED CRACKERS WITH ANCHOVIES

I tried a dish similar to this at a rooftop restaurant called Herb's Garden, in Heraklion, Crete, where they make crackers from *xinohondros*, a tangy mixture of wheat and soured milk. This version uses sour cream rather than *xinohondros* or equally hard-to-find sour milk and wheat *trahanas*. Raw fennel and anchovies are delicious on top. Rather than fennel seed, you can use black pepper, dried Greek oregano, chilli flakes, grated hard cheese or herbs such as chives in the crackers.

MAKES ABOUT 9 large crackers

CRACKERS
a little vegetable oil
70 g (2¼ oz/scant ⅔ cup) plain (all-purpose) flour, plus more to dust
1 heaped tablespoon sour (dairy sour) cream
scant ¼ teaspoon salt, or to taste
½ tablespoon fennel seeds
TO SERVE
¼ bulb of fennel, shaved or sliced very finely
18 marinated anchovies
pink peppercorns, crushed (optional)

Preheat the oven to 200°C (400°F/Gas 6). Lightly oil a baking sheet. Mix all the cracker ingredients together with 1–2 tablespoons of water, kneading with your hands until it makes a firm dough (or put all the ingredients in the food processor fitted with a dough blade and mix to a firm dough). Stop as soon as the dough comes together.

Dust a clean work surface with flour and roll out the dough until just under 5 mm (¼ in) thick. I prefer to cut the dough into rough rectangles with a knife, for a more rustic look, but you could also use a cookie cutter. Prick each cracker with a fork a couple of times. Transfer the crackers to the prepared baking sheet.

Place in the oven and bake for 15 minutes. (Check after 12 minutes, to ensure they are not browning too fast. If they are browning unevenly, turn the tray around.) Remove from the oven and cool.

Serve topped with shaved fennel, 2–3 anchovies and a few pink peppercorns (if using). Serve immediately.

TZATZIKI

For me, this cool, creamy and tangy yoghurt dip is a crucial part of any meze meal. It also makes a perfect sauce for grilled meats and is essential when serving souvlaki.

SERVES 4

200 g (7 oz/scant I cup) Greek yoghurt
¼ of a long cucumber, grated, excess liquid squeezed out
I garlic clove, crushed
I tablespoon finely chopped dill (dillweed)
½ teaspoon lemon juice, or to taste
I tablespoon extra-virgin olive oil, or to taste
salt and freshly ground black pepper

Line a sieve with muslin or paper towels, set it over a bowl and pour the yoghurt into it. Leave to drain for a couple of hours, or overnight, in the fridge. Discard the liquid.

   Add the cucumber, garlic and dill. Pour in the lemon juice and olive oil gradually, seasoning as you do so, tasting until the flavours are prefectly balanced. Chill until ready to serve.

AUBERGINE & SWEET PEPPER SALAD

This is a chunky version of a popular dip. If you prefer your *melitzanosalata* as a smooth dip, simply cook the aubergine (eggplant) whole in the same way as the pepper below (for full method, see page 48), then remove the skin and any large strands of seeds. Blitz all the ingredients together with 4–5 tablespoons of Greek yoghurt. Taste for seasoning and serve.

SERVES 4

1 red (bell) pepper
1 aubergine (eggplant), cut into 1 cm (½ in) slices, then quartered
2 garlic cloves, sliced
juice of ½ lemon
3 tablespoons olive oil
¼ teaspoon ground cumin
salt and freshly ground black pepper
2 tablespoons torn parsley leaves (optional)

Preheat the oven to 200°C (400°F/Gas 6).

Place the red pepper directly on to the naked flame of a gas ring and cook, turning regularly, for 10 minutes, or until blackened and charred all over. Remove from the heat and place in a sandwich bag. Seal and leave to cool. When cool enough to handle, remove from the bag and rub off and discard the skin.

Toss the aubergine, garlic, lemon juice, oil, cumin, salt and pepper together and tip into a baking sheet. Arrange so everything lies in a single layer. Place in the oven for 30 minutes, but check after 15. Turn the pieces of aubergine over and, if the garlic is cooking too quickly, remove and set aside (if it burns it will taste bitter).

Roughly chop the red pepper and strew on to a platter. Scatter over the parsley leaves (if using).

Remove the aubergine from the oven and allow to cool a little. Place the aubergine and garlic slices on the platter with the peppers and parsley, if used, and toss together gently. Best served at room temperature.

BROAD BEAN DIP

Broad (fava) beans are an important part of Greek culinary history: ancient Greek law-makers even used dried ones for voting. I love to change this dip by adding feta cheese, chopped fresh mint or a pinch of dried Greek oregano. It's also really good with chilli flakes stirred through or scattered on top.

SERVES 4
200 g (7 oz/1⅓ cups) fresh or frozen broad (fava) beans, shelled
salt
1 teaspoon lemon juice
1 garlic clove, finely chopped
2 tablespoons extra-virgin olive oil
1 shallot, finely sliced (optional)

Place the beans in a pan of boiling salted water. Return to the boil and cook for 2 minutes. Drain and refresh in cold water. Slip the beans out of their skins.

Place the skinned beans and all the other ingredients except the shallot in the food processor, or in a bowl and use a hand-held blender. Process until fairly smooth, but leave a little texture. To serve, scatter over the shallot slices (if using).

BURGHUL SALAÐ

This is a lovely salad, perfect for a lazy summer lunchtime. It is very adaptable. Try adding olives, preserved lemon, grilled courgette (zucchini) or chilli. A spoonful of Greek yoghurt makes a nice dressing.

SERVES 4

70 g (2¼ oz/⅓ cup) burghul (bulgur wheat)
150 g (5 oz) cucumber
150 g (5 oz) red and yellow tomatoes
¼–½ red onion
2 tablespoons finely chopped parsley leaves
juice of ½ lemon, or to taste
2½ tablespoons extra-virgin olive oil
plenty of salt and freshly ground black pepper
Greek yoghurt to serve (optional)

Cook the burghul according to the packet instructions. Allow to cool, then place in a mixing bowl.

Chop all the vegetables finely and add to the burghul with the parsley, lemon juice, oil and salt and pepper. Toss, then taste. Add more seasoning or lemon juice if necessary.

Transfer to a clean serving bowl. Serve with yoghurt, if you like.

SANTORINI SALAD

Versions of this wonderful salad are served all over the island of Santorini, an extraordinary place where white villages perch above steep cliffs that drop straight down into the sea. The cliffs are in fact part of the *caldera*, or crater edge, of a huge volcano, which in centuries past erupted violently and wiped out the island's population. (You can visit Pompeii-like excavations at Akrotiri.) The volcanic soil looks rough and barren, but actually means that Santorini's farmers can grow delicious vegetables and fruit without any irrigation at all, despite the scorching sun and hot winds which whip over cliff tops. Tomatoes, capers and caper leaves, split peas, cucumbers and grapes are particularly delicious.

SERVES 4

SALAD

1 Greek rusk (page 61) or 1 slice of wholemeal bread, or wholemeal bread roll

100 g (3½ oz) cucumber, halved and seeds scraped out

4–5 ripe tomatoes, depending on size, a mixture of yellow and red if possible, halved

2 spring onions (scallions), finely chopped

1 tablespoon capers or 3 sprigs of preserved caper leaves

200 g (7 oz) seasonal salad leaves: radicchio, watercress, mizuna, rocket (arugula) and amaranth all work well here

100 g (3½ oz) hard goats' cheese

DRESSING

3 tablespoons extra-virgin olive oil

1 tablespoon lemon juice

1 teaspoon finely chopped mint leaves

1 teaspoon finely chopped parsley leaves

1 teaspoon finely chopped dill (dillweed)

½ teaspoon dried Greek oregano

a little salt

If using a Greek rusk, break it into bite-sized pieces. If using bread or a roll, tear into bite-sized pieces and place in a low oven, preheated to 100°C (225°F/ Gas ¼), for 30 minutes to dry out and crisp up. Set aside.

Slice the cucumber into small pieces and place in a bowl with the tomatoes, spring onions, capers or caper leaves and salad leaves. Whisk together all the dressing ingredients, taste for seasoning, then pour half over the salad and toss.

Just before serving, roughly crumble the cheese and add it and the rusk or dried bread to the salad. Toss gently again, adding a little more dressing, if needed. Serve immediately.

GRAPE SALAD

This salad is based on one we were given at Nychteri, a lovely restaurant on Santorini run by the excellent chef Vassilis Zacharakis.

SERVES 4

SALAD
3 slices of pancetta, prosciutto, Serrano or Parma ham
1 teaspoon olive oil
8 grapes, halved
200 g (7 oz) seasonal salad leaves, radicchio, lollo rosso, rocket (arugula) or cos (romaine) lettuce all work well
50 g (2 oz) hard sheeps' cheese, such as Greek kefalotyri or young pecorino

DRESSING
1 teaspoon clear honey, or to taste
2 tablespoons extra-virgin olive oil
1 tablespoon lemon juice
salt and freshly ground black pepper

Tear the ham into bite-sized pieces. Pour the olive oil into a frying pan and cook the ham until crisp.

Whisk all the dressing ingredients together, taste and add more honey or seasoning as necessary.

Mix the ham, grapes and leaves together in a serving bowl. Pour half the dressing over the salad and toss to combine (you can add more dressing if needed). Crumble over the cheese. Serve immediately.

TARAMASALATA

There are dozens of ways to make *taramosalata*, a creamy dip made with fish eggs (roe), often carp or cod roe. It can be made with pungent smoked roe but, if so, soak the roe in cold water for a couple of hours beforehand to get rid of any bitterness. Some people like to add garlic, some garnish the dip with dill and others like to use mashed potatoes rather than soaked bread, but I think it's lighter made this way. How much roe to add depends on how strongly flavoured it is, so the below is only a guide.

SERVES 4

6 slices of day-old white bread, crusts removed
1 tablespoon lemon juice, or to taste
2 tablespoons extra-virgin olive oil
3 tablespoons cod or carp roe (smoked or unsmoked, or even canned), or to taste
1 shallot, grated
salt, to taste

Soak the bread in water then squeeze out thoroughly.

If you have a food processor or hand-held blender, blitz all the ingredients, taste, adjust the quantities of roe, salt or lemon juice and blitz again.

You can also make this in a mortar and pestle, which gives it a pleasing rustic look and chunky texture.

BROAD BEAN SALAD WITH MINT & PEA SHOOTS

This salad tastes of spring and the year's first broad beans are often eaten during Lent in Greece. Don't skip skinning the beans, it makes all the difference to the end result. If you want to make it heartier, add fresh blanched peas, goats' or sheeps' cheese, or curd cheese.

SERVES 4
200 g (7 oz/1⅓ cups) shelled fresh or frozen broad (fava) beans
pinch of salt and freshly ground black pepper
2 tablespoons extra-virgin olive oil
I teaspoon lemon juice
50–100 g (2–3½ oz) pea shoots
I tablespoon tiny or torn mint leaves

Place the beans in a pan of salted boiling water. Return to the boil and cook for 2 minutes. Drain and refresh in cold water. Pop the beans out of their skins.

Whisk the olive oil, lemon juice and salt and pepper together. Toss the pea shoots, skinned beans and mint together with half the dressing (you can add more as necessary). Serve straight away.

VINE LEAVES STUFFED WITH PORK

I learned this recipe for *yaprakia* from two wonderful black-clad older ladies on Rhodes, who were so practiced at wrapping vine leaves, they could do it without even looking.

MAKES ABOUT 30

40 vine leaves, preserved in brine
225 g (8 oz/1 cup) minced (ground) pork
4 spring onions (scallions), finely chopped
1 tomato, seeded and grated
160 g (5½ oz/¾ cup) risotto rice
½ teaspoon ground cumin
½ teaspoon salt
¼ teaspoon sweet paprika
½ teaspoon freshly ground black pepper
3 tablespoons finely chopped parsley leaves
1 tablespoon finely chopped mint leaves
1 teaspoon finely chopped dill (dillweed)
2 garlic cloves, finely chopped
juice of ½ lemon
2 tablespoons olive oil
Tzatziki (page 73) to serve

In a large pan of unsalted boiling water, blanch the vine leaves for 3 minutes to remove any salt. Remove and refresh in cold water. Set aside.

In a bowl, mix together all the other ingredients except the lemon juice and olive oil.

To stuff the leaves, place a whole, intact leaf on a flat surface with the stem end facing towards you. Remove the stem, if there is one. Place about 1 table-spoon of the pork mixture in the middle of the leaf, just above where the stem was. Lift the bottom sections of the leaf up and over the filling, then bring the side edges in over it too. Roll the leaf away from you, folding in and catching the edges of the leaf neatly into the roll as you go.

When you have rolled the whole leaf up, all the edges should be tucked into the roll and no filling should be visible.

Line a deep saucepan with any spare small, torn or broken vine leaves. Lay the stuffed vine leaves in layers, with the loose seam of the leaf on the bottom. Pack them in tightly so they can't unravel while cooking. When all the filling has been used up, drizzle over the lemon juice and olive oil and pour over enough water to just cover the wraps. Rest a plate or small saucepan lid on top to weigh them down, so they can't float loose while cooking.

Place the pan over a medium heat and bring to the boil, then reduce the heat and simmer for 30 minutes. Lift a stuffed leaf out the pan and allow to cool slightly. Open it up and taste to check that the rice has cooked. If not, simmer the wraps for 5 more minutes and test again.

When cooked, remove the wraps from the pan with a slotted spoon and allow to cool. Serve as part of a meze, with plenty of tangy tzatziki.

SELENE'S COURGETTE & SHRIMP FRITTERS

This recipe is based on one kindly given to me by Georgia Tsara from Selene restaurant on Santorini. Selene is easily one of the best places to eat on an island filled with great restaurants and amazing produce. Their version is served with their delicious home-made smoked cod's roe dip, Taramasalata (page 87). Using raw prawns gives a juicier result, but cooked prawns (thawed if frozen) will also work.

MAKES 8 fritters, enough for 2 as a main or 4 as a meze
pinch of salt
150 g (5 oz/generous 1 cup) grated courgette (zucchini),
1 egg, lightly beaten
1 teaspoon finely chopped dill (dillweed)
1 teaspoon finely chopped mint leaves
couple of grinds of freshly ground black pepper
50 g (2 oz) peeled raw sustainable cold water prawns, deveined
2 tablespoons day-old breadcrumbs, plus more if needed
2 tablespoons plain (all-purpose) flour
olive oil
Taramasalata (page 87) to serve (optional)
lemon juice to serve (optional)

Scatter the salt over the grated courgette and toss it all together. Set aside for 5 minutes, then squeeze the liquid out gently. Discard the liquid.

Add the egg, herbs and black pepper and mix. Then add the prawns, breadcrumbs and flour and stir. The mixture should just hold together. If not, add another tablespoon of breadcrumbs.

Put 1 cm (½ in) olive oil in a wide pan over a medium-high heat, warm. Drop 1 teaspoon of batter into the pan to see if the oil is hot enough: the batter should sizzle and brown fairly quickly. When cooked, taste to check the seasoning and adjust if necessary.

Carefully drop spoonfuls of the mixture into the oil and press gently to shape into patties. Cook in batches so you don't overcrowd the pan. Flip them over only when really golden on the bottom, after 2–3 minutes (any sooner and they may fall apart). Keep warm while you cook the rest.

Serve with taramasalata, especially one made with smoked roe, or a squeeze of lemon juice.

FISH & SEAFOOD

AS WITH ALL THE LOCAL
INGREDIENTS, EACH GREEK
ISLAND HAS ITS OWN
SPECIAL FISH DISHES,
LIKE THE PEARLY WRASSE
COOKED IN GARLIC IN
SOUTHERN RHODES OR
CORFU'S BIANCO SEAFOOD
STEW, BUT SOME DISHES ARE
COMMON TO ALMOST ALL
THE ISLANDS: CHARGRILLED
OCTOPUS; FRIED OR GRILLED
SARDINES; SHELLFISH
COOKED WITH FETA AND
TOMATOES; OR KAKAVIA, A
FISH SOUP THAT FISHERMEN
USED TO MAKE ON THEIR
BOATS USING THE SMALL
FISH THEY KNEW THEY
COULDN'T SELL THAT DAY.

CHARGRILLED OCTOPUS

Octopus is a staple of Greek island coastal cooking and you will often see little mesh-fronted boxes outside restaurants along the harbour, filled with octopus drying in the breeze. Drying them for a couple of days tenderises the meat, and the wire-framed boxes prevent local cats from making a feast of them. Octopus needs a long slow boil before char-grilling, otherwise it will be tough. Ask your fishmonger to prepare it for you by removing the head and mouth parts, as all you really want are the arms.

This recipe works just as well with frozen octopus as with fresh. It is easy to find in Spanish, Portuguese, Chinese or Asian stores if your fishmonger doesn't stock it.

SERVES 4 as a starter or meze
I raw octopus, usually 750 g–I kg (I lb 10 oz–2 lb 3 oz), defrosted if frozen, arms only
splash of olive oil, for cooking
2 tablespoons extra-virgin olive oil, for dressing
I tablespoon balsamic vinegar
freshly ground black pepper
¼ teaspoon dried Greek oregano
salt, if needed

Place the octopus arms in a large saucepan with a lid, turn the heat to high and bring to the boil without any added liquid, as it will release plenty of its own. Reduce the heat and simmer for I hour (you could add peppercorns, fennel seeds or coriander seeds if you fancy). Remove it from the liquid, drain and pat dry with paper towels.

Get a griddle pan hot over a high heat and add a splash of olive oil to grease the pan and the octopus. When charred all over, slice each piece on the diagonal into pieces about 5 mm (¼ in) thick.

Whisk together the extra-virgin olive oil, balsamic vinegar, black pepper and Greek oregano and use this to lightly dress the octopus. Taste to see if the dish needs a little salt. Serve warm or cool.

BAKED SARDINES

Sardines baked with Greek oregano are hugely popular across the islands as well as on the mainland. The addition of zingy capers, lemon and potatoes makes this a perfect one-pot supper.

SERVES 4

400 g (14 oz) baby new potatoes, scrubbed, skins on
8 very fresh sardines, gutted and scaled
4 tablespoons olive oil
1 tablespoon dried Greek oregano
3 garlic cloves, finely sliced
½ lemon, finely sliced
6 tablespoons lemon juice
2 teaspoons capers, rinsed
salt and freshly ground black pepper

Preheat the oven to 180°C (350°F/Gas 4).

Par-boil the new potatoes for 10 minutes, until just tender, then drain.

Place the sardines in a baking dish in which they will fit in a single layer once the potatoes are added. Tip in all the other ingredients, including the potatoes. Toss together and leave to marinate for 10 minutes.

Bake in the oven for 15 minutes, then serve immediately.

FISHERMAN'S PASTA

A lovely summery pasta dish, you'll find this served in harbour-side restaurants across Greece, populated by saucer-eyed kittens on the look-out for scraps from the diners. If you like a bit of spicy heat, add a pinch of dried chilli flakes. This recipe has a lot in common with prawn *saganaki*, which is really very similar, but made with ouzo instead of wine, and usually served with crusty bread rather than pasta.

SERVES 4

½ onion, finely chopped
pinch of salt
a little olive oil
1 garlic clove, finely chopped
1 tablespoon tomato purée (paste)
60 ml (2 fl oz/¼ cup) white wine
250 g (9 oz/1 cup) passata (sieved tomatoes) or blitzed canned tomatoes
pinch of dried Greek oregano
350 g (12 oz) dried spaghetti or linguine
1 medium squid, cleaned, body sliced into rings
4–8 raw sustainable cold water prawns, shelled and deveined
12 mussels
16 clams
75g (2½ oz) feta, crumbled
1 tablespoon roughly chopped parsley leaves

Sprinkle the onion with the salt. In a large pan with a lid, soften the onion in the olive oil over a medium-low heat for 10 minutes. Add the garlic and cook for a couple of minutes, stirring so that it doesn't stick, then add the tomato purée and cook for 2 minutes, again stirring all the time. Add the wine and cook for 5 minutes, then add the passata and the Greek oregano.

Meanwhile, bring a large saucepan of salted water to the boil. Put in the pasta and cook for a minute less than the packet suggests.

Cook the sauce for another 5 minutes, then increase the heat and add the squid, prawns and shellfish. Pop on the lid and cook for no more than 3 minutes.

Check that the seafood is cooked through, and discard any shells that have not opened. Stir in the feta, parsley and pasta, and serve.

ØCTØPUS PASTA

This is my twist on a Greek island and coastal favourite, *htapothi makaronatha*, octopus and tomato sauce served with short macaroni or ditalini. I love to use black squid ink pasta, which makes for a really dramatic-looking dish. This works just as well with frozen octopus as with fresh, which is easy to find in Spanish, Portuguese, Chinese or Asian stores, if your fishmonger doesn't stock it.

SERVES 2

200 g (7 oz) octopus arms, cooked or uncooked, defrosted if frozen
2 tablespoons olive oil, plus more for the octopus
1 small onion, finely chopped
small pinch of salt
2 garlic cloves, finely chopped
½ red chilli, seeded and finely chopped
2 tablespoons red wine
125 g (4 oz/½ cup) passata
½ teaspoon freshly ground black pepper
¼ teaspoon dried Greek oregano
200 g (7 oz) dried long pasta, such as linguine to serve
1 tablespoon chopped parsley leaves to serve

If you are starting with raw octopus arms, place them in a small saucepan with a lid, turn the heat to high and bring to the boil without any added liquid, as it will release plenty of its own. Reduce the heat and simmer for 1 hour, checking to ensure it hasn't boiled dry. Remove the octopus from the liquid, drain and pat dry with paper towels.

Once the octopus is cooked, heat a griddle pan with a little oil and grill the octopus, turning to char all sides, then slice it into 5 mm (¼ in) pieces.

Heat the 2 tablespoons of oil in a saucepan, and sauté the onion with the salt for 8–10 mins, until just soft and translucent. Next, add the garlic and the chilli, cook for 2 minutes, then add the wine. Let it bubble for a couple of minutes, then add the passata, pepper, Greek oregano and the cooked octopus and pour in 100 ml (3½ fl oz/scant ½ cup) of water.

Simmer for 15–20 minutes, until the mixture has a good sauce consistency. Taste and adjust the seasoning if necessary. Meanwhile, cook the pasta in boiling salted water until al dente. Drain.

At the last moment, stir the parsley into the sauce along with the cooked pasta.

MARINATED SARDINES

Lindos is a very beautiful old town of sugar lump-shaped white houses over-looked by an acropolis, on the coast of Rhodes. For more than seventy years, a restaurant called Mavrikos has been in the same family, set to the side of a busy square, and is now run by brothers Mihalis and Dimitris. This dish was just one of many glorious things that we ate there; perfectly fresh fish marinated in orange and lemon zests, fragrant coriander seeds and a sprinkling of fiery chilli, served with the local speciality: pickled samphire.

Don't be worried about butterflying sardines: it truly is simple.

SERVES 3–4 as a starter or meze

3 sardines
½ teaspoon chilli flakes, or to taste (optional)
½ teaspoon coriander seeds
¾ teaspoon salt
finely grated zest of ½ orange
finely grated zest of ½ lemon
2 tablespoons white wine vinegar
3–5 tablespoons extra-virgin olive oil

To butterfly the sardines: remove the head with a sharp knife. Starting at the head end, make an incision along the belly of the fish – not all the way through, just enough to break the skin – and allow the flesh to open up. Gently but firmly, pull out the guts and discard. Rinse the fish, then continue your incision down the fish to the tail, only allowing the knife to go as far as the spine. Snip the spine at this end with kitchen scissors. Working from the tail end, open up the fish like a book, and gently grasp the spine, leaving the tail intact. Pull the spine bones upwards, away from the flesh; most of the fine bones alongside it should come up and off, too.

Grind the chilli flakes (if using) and coriander seeds to a rough powder in a mortar and pestle.

Lay the sardines in a single layer in wide bowl, then scatter over the salt, the grated zests and the ground spices. Pour over the vinegar and turn the fish gently a couple of times to ensure they are well covered in marinade. Finally finish with the oil, using enough to cover the fish. Cover with plastic wrap and leave to mar-inate overnight in the fridge.

Drain off some of the marinade before serving. Slice the fish into smaller pieces, if you like.

WHITE FISH WITH GARLIC & LEMON

This dish was inspired by a lemon and garlic stew from Corfu called *bianco*, which because it is cooked with whole fish has a lovely richness to the sauce. However, it often contains sharp rogue bones. For this version, ask your fishmonger if you can keep the bones when the fish is filleted, then simmer them in the sauce for 10–15 minutes before carefully removing them. (This works even better if you tie the bones up in a piece of muslin.) This way, you get all the wonderful flavours without bones escaping into the sauce.

SERVES 2

5 tablespoons olive oil
5 fat garlic cloves, sliced
juice of 1 lemon
½ teaspoon freshly ground black pepper
¼ teaspoon salt
1 medium-sized white fish such as sea bass, mullet, bream, filleted, but keep the bones
200 g (7 oz) small waxy potatoes, cut into chunks
chopped parsley leaves to serve

Warm the oil in a wide pan over a medium heat. Add the garlic and cook for 1 minute. Pour in the lemon juice carefully, as it will spit, then follow with 250 ml (8 fl oz/1 cup) water. Add the pepper and salt and the fish bones to the pan, then the potatoes. Bring to the boil, reduce the heat to a simmer and cook for 30 minutes, with the lid half on. Keep an eye on the pan to ensure it doesn't dry out, but do allow the sauce to reduce.

Once the potatoes are cooked, remove the bones from the pan, checking none have escaped, then add the fish fillets. Cook in the sauce (there won't be much left by now) for 2–3 minutes, or until just cooked through. Stir in the parsley and serve immediately, making sure everyone gets plenty of the garlic.

SQUID BRAISED WITH GARLIC & ROSEMARY

Another dish inspired by the wonderful Mavrikos restaurant in Lindos, Rhodes (page 109).

SERVES 2 as a starter or 4 as a meze

4 tablespoons extra-virgin olive oil
8 garlic cloves, peeled and halved
pinch of salt, plus more if needed
200 g (7 oz) squid bodies and tentacles, cleaned and chopped into bite-sized pieces
1 tablespoon red wine
1 teaspoon rosemary leaves, finely chopped
¼ teaspoon balsamic vinegar (optional)

Place the olive oil in a heavy-based pan and warm it over a gentle heat. Add the garlic and the salt and cook slowly until the garlic is beginning to soften. Now add the squid and the wine. Cover and cook gently on a low heat for 30 minutes.

After 20 minutes of cooking, add the rosemary to the pan and replace the lid for the final 10 minutes.

At the end of cooking, taste, add more salt if necessary and stir in the balsamic vinegar (if using). Serve immediately.

CRISPY SQUID WITH BEETROOT SAUCE

Rather than the usual calamari with garlic mayonnaise, this combines earthy beetroot with saffron and lemon in a bright pink sauce.

SERVES 4 as a meze

SAUCE
100 g (3½ oz) raw beetroot (red beets), whole
pinch of saffron threads
1 tablespoon Greek yoghurt
salt and freshly ground black pepper
1 tablespoon lemon juice, or to taste

SQUID
100 g (3½ oz) squid bodies and tentacles
70 g (2¼ oz/geneorus ½ cup) plain (all-purpose) flour
½ teaspoon baking powder
salt and freshly ground black pepper
vegetable oil to fry
lemon wedges to serve

Preheat the oven to 200°C (400°F/Gas 6). Wrap the beetroots in foil and place in the oven for 1 hour, or until tender to the point of a knife. Remove from the foil and allow to cool. When cool enough to touch, rub off the skins with your thumbs.

Place the saffron in a cup and add 5 tablespoons of hot water. Leave to steep for 10 minutes. Strain, reserving the liquid, and blend it with the cooked beetroot and yoghurt, using a food processor or hand-held blender. Taste the sauce and add a little salt and lemon juice, to taste.

Meanwhile, slice the squid into rings and the tentacles into manageable pieces. Mix the flour, baking powder and some salt and pepper together and place it all in a sandwich bag. Add the squid to the bag and – holding the opening shut – give it a good shake. Let the squid sit in the flour for a couple of minutes. Remove the squid from the bag, shaking off excess flour.

Heat 3 cm (1¼ in) of vegetable oil to a large saucepan to 180°C (350°F) on a pan thermometer, or until a cube of bread browns in the oil in 30 seconds. Carefully drop the squid into the oil and fry quickly until golden brown, after just 30 seconds or so (otherwise it will be chewy). Remove with a slotted spoon and drain on paper towels. Serve the squid straightaway, with wedges of lemon to squeeze over and the beetroot sauce.

SALT COD FRITTERS

Served with potato skordalia on the side (page 191), as fried salt cod almost always is, this is essentially the Greek equivalent of British fish and chips, which may be why I like it so much! You can use either salt cod or fresh cod. In villages inland on the islands, dried salt cod meant that people who didn't live close to the coastlines could still eat fish. These fritters are delicious served with Beetroot salad (page 69) too.

SERVES 4

800 g (1 lb 12 oz) salt cod (or fresh cod, or other firm white fish)
250 ml (8½ fl oz/1 cup) lager or light ale
125 g (4 oz/1 cup) plain (all-purpose) flour
½ teaspoon baking powder
pinch of salt, if needed
vegetable oil for frying

If using salt cod, soak it in a bowl of cold water for 24 hours in the fridge, changing the water frequently to remove the salt. You can't use the fish until all the salt has been soaked out and rinsed away, or it will be overwhelmingly salty. The only way to know if you've reached the sweet spot is to taste the fish with the tip of your tongue. Alternatively, use fresh cod.

Whisk together the beer, flour and baking powder. It should form a batter about as thick as honey. If using fresh cod, add a little pinch of salt to the batter.

Rinse the cod for a final time. Remove any skin and large bones, then cut the fish into large chunks. Pat dry with paper towels.

Add about 3 cm (1¼ in) of vegetable oil to a large saucepan and set it over a medium-high heat. Heat it to 180°C (350°F) on a pan thermometer, or until a cube of bread browns in the oil in 30 seconds. Dredge the fish pieces in the batter and carefully lower into the oil, one or two at a time. Cook for 3–4 minutes, depending on the thickness of the fish. If the pieces are very chunky you may need to turn them carefully in the oil to ensure they brown and the fish cooks through. Remove with a slotted spoon and drain on paper towels. Serve immediately.

BREAM (OR ROSETIA) IN GARLIC SAUCE

At Perigiali on Stegna beach, Rhodes, the kitchen is famous for this dish. Rosetia is a kind of wrasse found in local waters, with extraordinary orange and pale pink scales. At Perigiali they cook it with garlic and red wine vinegar, pounded with breadcrumbs, and it is absolutely incredible. This version uses red or pink bream (although you could use any bream) as rosetia is almost never exported.

SERVES 2

5 garlic cloves, finely chopped
¼ teaspoon sea salt
1 slice day-old white bread, crusts removed, crumbled roughly
4 tablespoons olive oil, plus more to cook
2 tablespoons red wine vinegar
2 small whole red or pink bream, cleaned and gutted

Pound together the garlic, salt, bread, oil and vinegar in a large mortar and pestle until a pulpy sauce is achieved. Divide the sauce into quarters and smear a portion on to one side of each fish.

Get a wide frying pan hot over a medium-low heat. Add a splash of oil. Place both fish, coated side down, into the pan and cook gently for 4–5 minutes. Smear the rest of the coating onto the uncooked side. Turn and cook for 4–5 minutes longer, until the fish is cooked through and the coating golden and beginning to crisp up.

KAKAVIA
FISH SOUP

This is a very old recipe, found all over the Greek islands, for a fish stew originally made by fishermen as a way of using up fish that are too small to sell. Use whatever seasonal and sustainable fish or seafood you like the most.

SERVES 2

3 tablespoons olive oil
salt
I leek, finely chopped
I carrot, finely chopped
I celery stalk, finely chopped
300 g (10½ oz) potato, peeled and chopped into small bite-sized pieces
I ripe tomato, seeded and grated, skin discarded
I red mullet, gutted
juice of 2 lemons
freshly ground black pepper
2 sprigs of parsley
I courgette (zucchini), chopped into bite-sized pieces
200 g (7 oz) clams, cleaned
200 g (7 oz) mussels, cleaned

Get a wide pan (wide enough for the whole fish) hot over a medium heat. Add I tablespoon of olive oil and a pinch of salt and sauté the leek, carrot and celery for about 10 minutes, gently and without colouring.

Add the potato and grated tomato to the pan, then add ¼ teaspoon of salt and the remaining olive oil. Place the mullet on top of the potatoes, then pour in 350 ml (12 fl oz/1⅓ cups) of hot water, the lemon juice, some black pepper and the parsley sprigs. Reduce the heat to low, cover the pan and simmer for 20 minutes, or until the potatoes are tender.

Remove the mullet from the pan and discard the parsley. Gently pull the flesh from the bones of the fish. Discard the bones and keep the fish warm.

Add the courgette to the pan and cook for 5–7 minutes, until just beginning to soften.

Check over the clams and mussels. Discard any that are broken or open and will not close when firmly tapped.

Ensure the stew is simmering and add the mussels and clams to the pan. Clamp on the lid and cook for 3 minutes. Discard any shells that haven't opened after this time. Return the warm fish pieces to the pan and serve immediately, with plenty of crusty bread.

SQUID INK RISOTTO

This glorious and dramatic dish is another one inspired by a meal at Mavrikos restaurant in Lindos, Rhodes (page 109). It is unusual to find squid with its ink in the shops, and it is far easier (and less messy) to buy cleaned squid and sachets of the ink. Be sure to wear an apron and perhaps some plastic gloves when handling the ink, which stains.

SERVES 4

50 g (2 oz/½ stick) butter
I onion, very finely chopped
pinch of salt
4 garlic cloves, roughly chopped (optional)
300 g (10½ oz/1⅓ cups) risotto rice
120 ml (4 fl oz/½ cup) white wine
2 generous teaspoons or sachets of squid ink
650 ml (22 fl oz/2¾ cups) hot fish or vegetable stock, plus more if needed
100 g (3½ oz) squid, very finely chopped
lemon juice to taste
grated lemon zest to garnish

In a large pan, heat the butter until foaming, then add the onion, salt and garlic (if using). Cook for 5 minutes, stirring, do not allow to brown. Next, add the rice and cook, stirring, until each grain is coated in butter and beginning to become translucent. Add the wine and let it bubble. Then add the squid ink and stir well to make sure all the rice is coated with it.

When all the wine and squid ink has been absorbed by the rice, add a ladleful of hot stock. When the liquid has disappeared, add another. Continue in this way, stirring often or the rice will stick, for about 20 minutes. The rice is cooked when it is swollen and creamy and no longer white and firm. You may not need all the stock, or you may need a little more.

When the rice is cooked and just before serving, add the squid. (If you add the squid too soon, it will become tough.) After I minute, remove from the heat and stir in the lemon juice. Serve sprinkled with lemon zest.

LANGOUSTINES WITH ORZO

This feels, looks and is very luxurious, but frozen langoustines can be relatively inexpensive. You could also make it with halved lobsters, or use crayfish or lots of whole, unpeeled prawns. Orzo (risoni), or *kritharaki*, is widely used in Greek cooking.

SERVES 2

2 tablespoons olive oil
½ onion, grated
pinch of salt
2 garlic cloves, crushed
3 tablespoons white wine
200 g (7 oz/scant 1 cup) passata (sieved tomatoes)
¼ teaspoon sweet paprika
1 teaspoon red wine vinegar
freshly ground black pepper
knob of butter
75 g (2½ oz/⅓ cup) orzo (risoni) pasta
6 raw langoustines, defrosted if frozen

In a frying pan with a lid, warm the olive oil over a medium heat. Add the onion and salt and cook for 5 minutes, stirring all the time, until the onion is soft and translucent. Do not allow the onion to brown. Add the garlic and cook for 1 minute, then add the wine. Let bubble for a couple for minutes, then add the passata, paprika, vinegar and a generous grind of black pepper. Simmer on a very low heat for 15 minutes, adding a little water if it seems as though it might dry out.

Meanwhile, melt the butter in a small pan and, when it is foaming, add the orzo. Sauté, stirring constantly, for a couple of minutes until golden. Tip the contents of the orzo pan into the tomato pan and add about 75 ml (2½ fl oz/ ⅓ cup) of water. Bring to a simmer, then cook for a couple of minutes.

Snip the antennae from the langoustines and discard them. Lay the langoustines on top of the sauce, add 50 ml (2 fl oz/¼ cup) of water and clamp the lid on. Increase the heat to low medium and cook for 7 minutes, or until the langoustines are cooked (the flesh will turn white). Serve immediately, with plenty of napkins.

SEA BASS WITH COURGETTE SAUCE

This is another recipe inspired by one given to me by Georgia Tsara from Selene restaurant on Santorini. Their incredible version of this dish also contains courgette flowers and beautiful burghul croquettes, and I certainly recommend making a pilgrimage to the restaurant to try it (see page 254).

The courgette sauce may be very simple but is packed with fresh spring-like flavours and would work with any white fish. I like to serve it with chicory (Belgian endive), fennel and pea shoots, cooked for a minute or two in a little butter.

SERVES 4

¼ fennel bulb
I lemon, halved
⅛ tsp salt
I large courgette (zucchini), about 300 g (IO oz), grated
40g (I½ oz/ 3 tablespoons) butter, plus more for the fish
90–IOOml (3–3½ fl oz/⅓–½ cup) single (light) cream
I tablespoon mint leaves
salt and freshly ground black pepper
4 fillets sustainably-sourced sea bass or other sustainable white fish fillets
50–60g (2 oz/I¾ cups) pea shoots
head of chicory (Belgian endive), leaves separated

Finely slice the fennel bulb, then toss with a little lemon juice to prevent discolouration. Set aside.

Scatter the salt over the grated courgette and toss it all together. Set aside for 5 minutes, then squeeze the liquid out of the courgette gently (discard the liquid).

Melt 30 g (I oz/ 2 tablespoons) of the butter in a pan set over a low heat and add the courgette. Cook very gently until soft, stirring often; do not allow the courgette to brown. Reduce the heat to the lowest possible, then add 90 ml (3 fl oz/ ⅓ cup) of the cream to the pan and simmer very gently for 3–4 minutes.

Place the mint leaves in a little boiling water and let stand for 30 seconds. Strain, then tear the leaves into pieces and add them to the pan. Using a hand-held blender, blend to form a smooth sauce. If it seems too thick, add a little more cream. Taste and adjust the seasoning if necessary. Cover and keep the sauce warm while you cook the fish.

Melt a little butter in a pan wide enough to take all the fillets. Season the fish lightly and place, skin side-down, in the pan. Reduce the heat to medium-low and cook for about 3 minutes, until the skin is golden brown, turn and cook the other side for a minute or two, until the fish is just cooked.

Meanwhile, melt the remaining 15 g (½ oz/1 tablespoon) of butter in a wide pan over a gentle heat. Add the fennel, pea shoots and chicory and cook, stirring, until just coated in butter and beginning to wilt. Remove from the heat.

Spoon the sauce into warm bowls. Top with the buttered vegetables then lay the fish on top, skin side up.

FAVA & MUSSEL RISOTTO

I tried this unusual risotto at a seaside restaurant on Santorini, expecting a risotto studded with fresh broad (fava) beans. But – happily – this was what arrived: a risotto with fava purée stirred through, which makes it very hearty and filling. You could use prawns instead of mussels in this risotto, if you prefer.

SERVES 2

pinch of saffron threads
50 g (2 oz/½ stick) butter
½ onion, finely chopped
1 tomato, seeded and chopped
pinch of salt
1 garlic clove, finely chopped
½ teaspoon tomato purée (paste)
300 g (10½ oz/1⅓ cups) risotto rice
120 ml (4 fl oz/½ cup) white wine
about 500 ml (17 fl oz/2¼ cups) hot fish or vegetable stock
5 tablespoons Fava dip (page 43)
8 mussels, cleaned, or more if small

Put the saffron in a cup and add 2 tablespoons of boiling water. Set aside.

In a large pan, heat the butter until foaming, then add the onion, tomato, salt, garlic and tomato purée. Cook for 5 minutes, stirring, and do not allow to brown.

Next, add the rice and cook, stirring, until each grain is coated in the tomato and butter mixture and is beginning to become translucent. Add the wine and let it bubble. When it has all been absorbed by the rice, add a ladleful of hot stock. When the liquid has disappeared, add another. Continue in this way, stirring often or the rice will stick, for about 20 minutes. The rice is cooked when it is swollen and creamy and no longer white and firm. You may not need all the stock, or you may need a little more.

When the rice is almost cooked, strain the saffron liquid into the risotto and stir, then add the fava dip and stir again. Reduce the heat to its lowest. Finally, add the mussels, stir, then clamp on the lid. Stir again after 1½ minutes, replace the lid, then stir again after a further 1½ minutes. Discard any mussels that haven't opened. Serve immediately.

MEAT

MANY PEOPLE EXPECT GREEK ISLAND COOKING TO BE ALL ABOUT FISH, BUT MEAT IS VERY IMPORTANT, ESPECIALLY TO PEOPLE LIVING IN THE OFTEN MOUNTAINOUS AND REMOTE INTERIORS OF ISLANDS LIKE CRETE AND RHODES, WHERE GOATS AND SHEEP ROAM FREELY. GAME HAS BEEN HUNTED HERE FOR THOUSANDS OF YEARS, AND FAMILY RECIPES USING RABBITS, WILD BIRDS AND VENISON ARE PASSED DOWN THROUGH THE GENERATIONS. MEAT IS OFTEN SLOW COOKED, SOMETIMES IN WOOD OVENS AS THEY COOL OVERNIGHT, LIKE LAMB WITH CHICKPEAS, OR IT MAY BE STEWED WITH ONIONS, LIKE RABBIT STIFADO.

CHICKEN IN RED WINE SAUCE WITH PASTA

I first tried this dish, *kotopoulo me hilopites*, made with a rooster rather than chicken, on Santorini, but it is similar to a famous celebratory dish from Corfu, *pastitsatha*, which is often cooked with spicy hot peppers and with veal, beef or even seafood instead of chicken. This makes a delicious and easy weeknight supper.

To grate fresh tomatoes, place a box grater in a sieve, then place both inside a large bowl to catch the juice. Put a folded tea towel under the bowl to stop it slipping. Cut the tomatoes in half across the middle and place the cut surface against the grater. Grate, using the skin to protect your hands. Discard the skins.

SERVES 2

2 tablespoons olive oil
450 g (1 lb) skinless boneless chicken thighs, cut into bite-sized pieces
1 onion, finely chopped
2 garlic cloves, finely chopped
1 tablespoon tomato purée (paste)
200 ml (7 fl oz/scant 1 cup) red wine
200 g (7 oz/scant 1 cup) canned chopped tomatoes, or 4 very ripe, fresh tomatoes, halved, seeded and grated, skins discarded
3 cm (1¼ in) cinnamon stick
⅛ teaspoon ground allspice
2 bay leaves
salt and freshly ground black pepper
200 g (7 oz) dried long pasta, such as tagliatelle
grated or shaved kefalotyri or pecorino cheese to serve

Set a wide pan over a fairly high heat, add the oil and brown the chicken pieces thoroughly, in batches, otherwise they will stew rather than brown. Remove the first batch to a plate while you brown the rest. Return all the meat to the pan, reduce the heat and add the onion. Cook gently, stirring often, for 8–10 minutes, then add the garlic and cook for 2 minutes, stirring again.

Add the tomato purée and cook for a further 2 minutes, stirring. Next, deglaze the pan by adding the red wine, scraping up any bits that have stuck to the pan. Add the tomatoes, cinnamon, allspice, bay leaves and 100 ml (3½ fl oz/scant ½ cup) of hot water and season generously. Stir, reduce the heat and simmer for 35 minutes, partially covered with a lid, stirring occasionally.

When the sauce is nearly ready and most the liquid has reduced, cook the pasta in boiling salted water for 1 minute less than the packet instructions.

Taste the sauce and adjust the seasoning if necessary. Discard the bay leaves. Serve the sauce mixed with the pasta or stirred though, with a little cheese scattered over each bowl.

SLOW-COOKED LAMB WITH CHICKPEAS

This recipe is based on one of a series of incredible dishes we tasted at To Limeri Tou Listi, a rustic little restaurant in a tiny mountain village called Profilia on the island of Rhodes. The owner, Savvas, and his wife kindly showed me how to cook a few of their dishes, which are famous among locals. They make this dish with goat and slow-cook it overnight after the restaurant closes, as their outside wood oven cools.

If you can get hold of goat, all the better, just treat it exactly the same way as the lamb below. You could also use mutton. Slow cooking isn't an exact science, so the timings below are guidelines only; you may find that some cuts or types of meat need a little longer. It's the kind of dish best suited to leaving in the oven with the lid on while you go for a walk on a Sunday afternoon.

SERVES 4 with leftovers

2–3 tablespoons olive oil
800 g (1 lb 12 oz) stewing lamb in large pieces: shanks, fore shanks or shoulder are all good
2 onions, chopped
400 g (14 oz) can of cooked chickpeas (garbanzos)
1 tablespoon tomato purée (paste)
120 ml (4 fl oz/½ cup) red wine
2 x 400 g (14 oz) cans chopped tomatoes
½ teaspoon ground allspice
salt and freshly ground black pepper

Preheat the oven to 140°C (275°F/Gas 1).

In a large, wide, flameproof and ovenproof pan with a lid, heat 2 tablespoons of the oil and brown the meat thoroughly, in batches otherwise it will stew rather than brown. Remove the meat from the pan, reduce the heat and add the remaining oil, if necessary. Soften the chopped onions in the pan for 10 minutes, stirring often. Meanwhile, remove the skins from the chickpeas by rubbing them off with your fingers.

Next, add the tomato purée to the pan and cook, stirring, for 2 minutes. Then add the wine, stirring and scraping with a wooden spoon as it bubbles to get up any bits that have stuck to the pan. After 2 minutes, add the tomatoes, browned meat, chickpeas, allspice and 500 ml (17 fl oz/2¼ cups) of hot water to the pan. Season generously, return to the boil, stir, then clamp the lid on and place in the oven. Cook for 2½ hours, then uncover and cook for a final hour. By this

point, much of the liquid will have reduced and the meat will be falling apart. If the meat is still tough, return to the oven; if there's still too much liquid, remove from the oven, place on the hob and simmer to reduce. Taste the sauce before serving and adjust the seasoning, if necessary.

Serve with crusty bread and some seasonal greens.

VØLCANIC LAMB WITH EGG & LEMØN SAUCE

This dish was inspired by a restaurant called Sirocco on the island of Milos. Rather than cooking with a conventional oven, each night the Tseroni family bury dishes full of lamb, pork, aubergines or potatoes in a patch of hot volcanic sand on the beach beside their blue-painted restaurant terrace. This simple recipe is how the chef, Stella Tseroni, cooks lamb, although she leaves hers in the low and steady heat underground for seven hours. I wasn't sure that it was possible to cook lamb with so little liquid, but she assured me the meat would produce its own broth and she was right.

The zesty lemon sauce is called *avgolemono* and can be made with any kind of stock, or used in soups. It is delicious when made with fish stock and drizzled over grilled whole fish.

SERVES 4

LAMB
I onion, sliced
I tablespoon olive oil
4 lamb shanks, weighing 300 g–400 g (10½–14 oz) each
6 sprigs of thyme, plus more to serve
salt and freshly ground black pepper
400 g (14 oz) baby new potatoes, in their skins
a little butter

SAUCE
I egg
juices from the lamb
I tablespoon lemon juice, or to taste

Preheat the oven to 140°C (275°F/Gas I).

For the lamb, soften the onion gently in a wide pan with the olive oil. Increase the heat and add the lamb, browning the shanks thoroughly on all sides. Deglaze the pan with 4–5 tablespoons of water, scraping up any bits that have stuck. Tip the whole lot into an ovenproof dish with a tight-fitting lid and add the thyme, salt and pepper. Place the lid on the dish and put into the oven. Cook for 3 hours, or until the meat is falling from the bone.

Just before the lamb comes out of the oven, boil the new potatoes in salted water until just tender. Drain and dry on paper towels then sauté gently in the butter over a medium-low heat, until lightly browned all over.

When the lamb is cooked, spoon off most of the juices from the dish, leaving just enough so the meat doesn't dry out. Keep it somewhere warm, with the lid on.

Make the sauce. Beat the egg until creamy. Very slowly drizzle in the hot pan juices, whisking constantly to ensure the egg doesn't cook and make the sauce lumpy, then add the lemon juice. Pour it all into a clean pan and warm over a very, very gentle heat, but do not bring anywhere close to boiling. If you feel there isn't enough sauce, add a little stock or even water. You can also add more lemon juice, to taste. Remove from the heat and serve with the lamb, onions and potatoes, scattered with a few thyme leaves.

MØUSSAKA

This dish can be a controversial subject among Greek cooks, as everyone thinks they know the best way of making it (or if they don't then their mother does), so I was careful to ask lots of chefs and cooks as I tried to work out my favourite version. (I learned a lot from a wonderful lady in a shoe shop one afternoon, after my sandals broke.) I like a fairly deep layer of béchamel on the top of my moussaka and I prefer to make it with minced beef, or beef and veal. However, it can be very good made with lamb, in which case a little pinch of cinnamon can really elevate the flavour. If you are a cheese lover, you might like to grate a little cheese on top, just before serving.

SERVES 4

BÉCHAMEL
60 g (2 oz/½ stick) butter
60 g (2 oz/½ cup) plain (all-purpose) flour
800 ml (27 fl oz/3⅓ cups) hot milk
salt and freshly ground black pepper
freshly grated nutmeg
20 g (¾ oz/¼ cup) grated pecorino or parmesan, or the Greek hard sheeps' milk cheese, kefalotyri
1 egg, beaten

FILLING
2 large aubergines (eggplants)
400 g (14 oz) waxy potatoes
splash of olive oil, plus more for the aubergines, the meat and the dish
500 g (1 lb 2 oz/2¼ cups) minced (ground) lamb, beef, or veal
1 onion, finely chopped
2 garlic cloves, crushed
1 teaspoon tomato purée (paste)
160 ml (5½ fl oz/scant ¾ cup) red wine
200 g (7 oz/scant 1 cup) passata (sieved tomatoes) or blitzed canned tomatoes
1 tablespoon finely chopped parsley leaves
½ teaspoon dried Greek oregano

Make the béchamel: melt the butter over a low heat and add the flour. Mix and cook very gently for 2–3 minutes. Gradually add the hot milk, little by little (too much at a time and the sauce will become lumpy). Continue to cook, stirring often, for 10 minutes, on the lowest possible heat, until the sauce becomes glossy. Season with salt, pepper and a generous grating of nutmeg, then stir in the grated cheese. Allow to cool for a few minutes, then slowly pour in the egg, whisking vigorously as you do so (make sure the béchamel really is cool enough first, otherwise the egg will scramble). Cover and set aside.

Preheat the oven to 200°C (400°F/Gas 6) then prepare the filling. Slice the aubergines into rounds about 5 mm (¼ in) thick, then place them in a colander. Scatter with a pinch of salt, toss gently and leave to drain over the sink for 10 minutes.

Meanwhile peel the potatoes and slice into rounds of the same size as the aubergine. Heat the oil in a wide pan and gently fry the potatoes until just beginning to colour, then set aside.

Brush a baking tray with olive oil. Pat the aubergine slices dry with paper towels and place them on the baking sheet. Brush the slices with olive oil and place in the oven for 15 minutes. Turn over and return to the oven for 5–10 minutes, or until just beginning to brown. Set aside.

In a clean pan, brown the minced meat really thoroughly over a high heat with a splash of oil, stirring until all the grains are separate. (You may need to do this in batches, as if the pan is crowded the meat will stew rather than brown.) Remove the meat and set aside, then add the onion to the pan and cook gently to soften (add a little more oil if necessary), for 10 minutes or so, stirring to prevent it from sticking. Add the garlic and tomato purée and cook, stirring, for 2 minutes. Return the minced meat to the pan and add the wine. Let bubble, using a wooden spoon to scrape any bits from the pan. After a couple of minutes, add the tomatoes and herbs, then pour in 200 ml (7 fl oz/¾ cup) of water. Simmer for 15 minutes. Taste and season.

To assemble the moussaka, oil a large, high-sided ovenproof dish, and line the base with the potatoes. Pour over the meat sauce, then cover with the aubergine slices. Pour the béchamel evenly over the aubergine. Bake in the oven for 55 minutes, until deep golden brown on top.

Leave to stand for 10 minutes before serving. Don't serve moussaka piping hot, as it may fall apart.

Photograph overleaf

PØRK
MEATBALLS

These are very tasty, served with a hearty sauce. As with so many Greek dishes, there are dozens of variations to this *keftedes* dish, some using mint, orzo or cinnamon, so feel free to experiment.

SERVES 4

MEATBALLS
I small onion
I spring onion (scallion)
2 garlic cloves
a handful of parsley leaves
350 g (12 oz/1½ cups) minced (ground) pork (not too lean)
½ teaspoon dried Greek oregano
¾ teaspoon salt
I teaspoon freshly ground black pepper
2 slices of white bread, crusts discarded
a little milk
butter or olive oil for frying

SAUCE
4 tablespoons olive oil
I onion, finely chopped
pinch of salt
2 garlic cloves, finely chopped
100 ml (3½ fl oz/scant ½ cup) red wine
¼ teaspoon allspice
½ teaspoon freshly ground black pepper
½ teaspoon sweet paprika
200 g (7 oz/scant I cup) passata (sieved tomatoes)

For the meatballs, in a food processor or by hand, chop the onions, garlic and parsley very finely. Then, using your hands, mix this with the pork, Greek oregano, salt and pepper. Soak the bread in the milk for 5 minutes, then squeeze out the milk and mash the bread to a pulp. Add to the meatball mixture. Mix thoroughly and set aside, covered, for about 30 minutes.

To make the sauce, warm the olive oil in a large pan over a low heat. Add the onion and salt and cook for 8 minutes, then add the garlic and cook for a further 2 minutes. Increase the heat, pour in the wine and allow to bubble for a couple of minutes. Add the allspice, black pepper and paprika and cook, stirring, for a couple of minutes. Add the passata and bring to a gentle simmer, cooking for 15 minutes. Keep checking and if the sauce is too dry, add a splash of hot water.

Meanwhile, shape the meat mixture into balls. You should be able to make about 16. Cook the meatballs in a wide pan over a medium-high heat, with a little butter or a splash of olive oil, until browned all over and cooked through. Turn them gently at the beginning of the cooking process, otherwise they may fall apart; they beome more robust as they cook further. When cooked, transfer to the pan with the sauce and toss gently to coat. Serve with rice or crusty bread, Wilted greens (page 192) or Green herb salad (page 66).

MEAT

SMOKED PORK IN A CREAMY SAUCE

Apakia, a kind of smoked pork, is a Cretan speciality, but when I can't use the real thing, I use smoked gammon instead. This is a creamy pork dish which is easy to make but feels rich and indulgent. Often this is served with rice, but I prefer it with some crusty bread and a fresh-tasting Green herb salad (page 66).

SERVES 2

320 g (11 oz) smoked pork, in bite-sized chunks
olive oil
1 onion, finely sliced
100 ml (3½ fl oz/scant ½ cup) white wine
2 teaspoons sun-dried tomato purée (paste)
60 g (2 oz/¼ cup) mascarpone
1 tablespoon finely chopped parsley leaves
freshly ground black pepper

Get a pan hot over a medium heat and very lightly brown the pork in a little oil. Add the onion and cook gently for 10 minutes, until soft. Pour in the wine and scrape up any browned bits from the pan. Bubble the wine for 8–10 minutes, then pour in 100 ml (3½ fl oz/scant ½ cup) hot water, cover and reduce the heat to its lowest. Let simmer for 25 minutes or until the meat is really tender. Remove the lid for the last 5 minutes to allow the liquid to reduce.

Remove from the heat and stir in the sun-dried tomato purée, mascarpone, parsley and pepper. Return to the heat and slowly bring back to the boil, simmering for a final couple of minutes before serving with rice or crusty bread and a herb salad.

SLOW-COOKED VENISON WITH WHEAT BERRIES

Cooking with wheat was a technique used by some cooks to preserve meat during the Second World War. Meat would be cooked and the wheat berries mixed with the fat that rose to the top of the dish, sealing it and preserving it for up to a few months. On the island where I first ate this dish, it is illegal to hunt deer, and I was told it was beef...which it definitely was not.

SERVES 4

700 g (1 lb 8 oz) stewing venison, diced
4 tablespoons plain (all-purpose) flour
a little olive oil
2 onions, finely chopped
2 carrots, finely chopped
2 celery stalks, finely chopped
4–6 garlic cloves, to taste, finely chopped
120 ml (4 fl oz/½ cup) red wine
400 g (14 oz/1½ cups) passata (sieved tomatoes)
½ teaspoon salt
½ teaspoon freshly ground black pepper
1 teaspoon dried Greek oregano
2 teaspoons thyme leaves
leaves from 2 sprig of rosemary, finely chopped
125 g (4 oz/⅔ cup) wheat berries
chopped parsley leaves to serve

Preheat the oven to 140°C (275°F/Gas 1). Dust the venison with the flour. Using an ovenproof casserole dish, brown the venison over a fairly high heat in the oil, in batches, as overcrowding the pan will result in stewed rather than browned meat, which will give the stew less flavour. Remove the meat from the pan once it is browned and set aside. In the same pan, reduce the heat to its lowest and cook the onions gently for 8–10 minutes until just beginning to brown. Then add the carrots, celery and garlic and cook for a further 5 minutes. Add the wine and deglaze the pan, scraping any burnt bits off the base.

Return the meat to the pan, add the passata and cook for 5 minutes. Add the salt, pepper and herbs, then 600 ml (1 pint/2½ cups) of water. Return to the boil, then put the lid on the casserole and place in the oven. Cook for 2 hours. The meat should be almost falling apart.

Add the wheat berries and 120 ml (4 fl oz/½ cup) of water (or less if the pan is very full of liquid), stir, and return to the oven.

Cook for a further 25–45 minutes, checking the pan occasionally. The dish is ready when the wheat has softened and a chunk of the meat can be pulled apart with a spoon. Stir in the parsley. Serve with wilted greens or a crisp salad.

CHICKEN SOUVLAKI

The word *souvlaki* simply means to cook something on a skewer, something Greek cooks have been doing for thousands of years: cooking skewers were found during excavations on Santorini which date back to the seventeenth century BC. They can be made with pork, beef, lamb, chicken or even vegetables. I love to make them with chicken and plenty of tzatziki and red onion.

When rolling up a wrap, fold the bottom of the flatbread up slightly, to stop the filling falling out, then roll in from the sides.

MAKES 4 souvlaki wraps

CHICKEN AND MARINADE
300 g (10 oz) skinless chicken breasts
1 teaspoon sweet paprika
1 teaspoon dried Greek oregano
2 garlic cloves, crushed
1 tablespoon lemon juice
1 teaspoon red wine vinegar
salt and freshly ground black pepper
1 tablespoon olive oil

SOUVLAKI
a little olive oil
½ courgette (zucchini), shaved or sliced into thin strips
4 warm Flatbreads (page 32)
Tzatziki (page 73)
½ red onion, finely sliced

Place the chicken in a bowl with all the other marinade ingredients. Cover and leave in the fridge for at least 2 hours, preferably overnight.

Preheat the grill (broiler) to maximum. Thread the meat on to metal skewers, then grill for 3–5 minutes each side, until cooked through.

Meanwhile, heat a griddle or frying pan over a high heat with a little oil. Griddle the courgette until just beginning to brown, just a minute or 2. Stack each flatbread with tzatziki, chicken, courgette and a little onion. Roll up and eat immediately.

PHEASANT PASTA

In the mountainous interior of many of the Greek islands, hunting for game is very popular, regardless of whether it is technically allowed or not. Slow-cooked game birds such as pheasant make a wonderful sauce for Greek pasta.

Cooking the meat with bones in and removing them later makes for a richer and more flavoursome sauce but, if you prefer, you or your butcher can de-bone the bird before cooking.

SERVES 2

4 tablespoons olive oil
I pheasant, jointed, with bones
I carrot, finely chopped
I celery stalk, finely chopped
I onion, finely chopped
6 garlic cloves, chopped
I tablespoon tomato purée (paste)
120 ml (4 fl oz/½ cup) red wine
leaves from I sprig of thyme
leaves from ½ sprig of rosemary, finely chopped
⅛ teaspoon dried Greek oregano
I teaspoon cider vinegar
salt and freshly ground black pepper
200 g (7 oz) dried long pasta, such as tagliatelle
I tablespoon pine nuts to serve (optional)
chopped parsley leaves to serve

Get a wide pan hot over a medium-high heat. Add I tablespoon of the olive oil and brown the pheasant really thoroughly until golden brown all over. You may need to do this in batches, otherwise it will stew rather than brown.

Remove the meat from the pan and set aside. Reduce the heat under the pan to low. Add the carrot, celery, onion and garlic. Cook for 8 minutes, just long enough for the vegetables to take on a little colour and soften. Next, add the tomato purée and cook, stirring often, for 3 minutes.

Deglaze the pan by pouring in the wine. Turn the heat up and let it bubble for a couple of minutes, scraping the base of the pan with a wooden spoon. Then return the meat to the pan, and pour in 375 ml (13 fl oz/1½ cups) of water (or a little more if necessary) to cover. Add the herbs, vinegar and a generous grinding of salt and pepper. Once it has returned to the boil, cover and reduce the heat to a simmer. Cook for an hour, or until the meat is really tender. Remove all the meat from the pan and pick it from the bones (you may like to

warn your guests that small pieces of bone may remain!). Return the meat to the pan. Add 150 ml (5 fl oz/½ cup) boiling water and the uncooked pasta. Stir. Cook, with the lid on, stirring once or twice, until the pasta is al dente (how long exactly will depend on what sort of pasta you choose). Keep an eye on the pot and add 1–2 tablespoons of water if it starts to stick to the bottom. Meanwhile toast the pine nuts (if using) in a dry pan for 2–3 minutes, until golden. To serve, stir in the parsley and scatter the pine nuts on top.

RABBIT STIFADO

Stifado is a wonderful Greek stew that is always made with lots of tiny onions and sometimes with tomato; this version is rich and aromatic with spices but if you prefer a sharper flavour, add half a can of chopped tomatoes after the wine. Rabbit can take anything from one to three hours to cook, depending on the age of the rabbit and whether it is wild or not, so, sometimes it might be best to cook it in advance and reheat it to serve. Stifado can also be made with chicken, game birds, even goat or venison, if you prefer. Serve with Lemon, garlic and herb roasted potatoes (page 188) and a green salad with a sharp dressing, to cut through the richness.

SERVES 4

olive oil to cook
1 whole rabbit, skinned and jointed, without offal
15 small onions
6 garlic cloves
1 tablespoon tomato purée (paste)
250 ml (8½ fl oz/1 cup) red wine
1 teaspoon red wine vinegar
1 bay leaf
3 cm (1¼ in) cinnamon stick
leaves from ½ sprig of rosemary, finely chopped
¼ teaspoon freshly ground black pepper
salt

Preheat the oven to 160°C (325°F/Gas 3).

In a large ovenproof pan with a lid, warm 1 tablespoon of olive oil over a high heat. Place half the rabbit pieces into the pan and brown thoroughly, then remove from the pan and set aside. Do the same with the other half. Add the onions and garlic and fry for 3 minutes, stirring, just long enough for them to get a little colour. Add the tomato purée and cook for 2 minutes, stirring again. Add the red wine and deglaze the pan: let the wine bubble and stir, scraping up any burnt on bits from the base and sides. Add the vinegar, bay leaf, cinnamon stick and rosemary, stir, then return the meat to the pan.

Add 500 ml (17 fl oz/2¼ cups) of hot water and the pepper, plus a generous grinding of salt. Bring to the boil, cover and place in the oven. Cook for 1 hour, then check to see if the meat is becoming tender; if not, return to the oven for 30 minutes. Continue to check every 30 minutes until the meat is falling off the bones; this may take as long as 3 hours.

When the meat is tender, remove the pan from the oven. Take the meat out of the pan and set aside. Remove and discard the cinnamon. Place the pan over a medium heat and reduce the liquid left in the pan until thickened and saucy (this may not need to be done if the meat has been in the oven for a very long time).

MEAT

CHICKEN BAKED IN YOGHURT

Sweet slow-roasted shallots and garlic are delicious with chicken and this tangy yoghurt sauce.

SERVES 4

knob of unsalted butter
8 free-range chicken thighs and drumsticks, or 4 whole leg portions
16 spring onions (scallions)
juice of 1 lemon
salt and freshly ground black pepper
16 shallots, quartered
8 garlic cloves, chopped into chunks
250 g (9 oz/1 cup) Greek yoghurt
2 teaspoons finely chopped dill (dillweed)
2 eggs, beaten
4 tablespoons grated pecorino or Greek kefalotyri cheese

Preheat the oven to 200°C (400°F/Gas 6).

Place the butter in a frying pan over a medium heat. Add the chicken and brown it all over. Trim and cut the spring onions into 2 cm (¾ in) lengths and place in an ovenproof dish which will fit all the ingredients snugly. Pour in the lemon juice and then the contents of the chicken pan, including the hot fat. Season with salt and pepper, then add the shallots and garlic and toss them in the fat. Arrange the chicken so it is resting on the shallots, place in the oven and cook for 30 minutes, basting halfway through cooking.

Meanwhile, mix together the yoghurt, dill, eggs and cheese and season with a little salt and pepper.

After the chicken has cooked for 30 minutes, remove from the oven and pierce a thigh to the bone to check it is cooked through; the meat should come away from the bone and the juices should run clear. If not, return to the oven for 5–10 minutes. When cooked, pour over the yoghurt mixture and return to the oven for 15 minutes, to allow the sauce to thicken and begin to brown.

Serve immediately with a green salad.

ÐRUNKEN CHICKEN

This dish, *methisméno kotopónlo*, can be found on menus all over Greece, and simply means the chicken was cooked with alcohol. This is my favourite version. If you can't find ouzo, any other aniseed liquor will work, even absinthe or pastis.

SERVES 3–4

3 free-range whole chicken leg portions
2 tablespoons ouzo or other aniseed liquor
60 ml (2 fl oz/¼ cup) olive oil
60 ml (2 fl oz/¼ cup) white wine
2 tablespoons lemon juice, plus more to serve
½ teaspoon clear honey
6 shallots or small onions, quartered
3 garlic cloves, cut into chunks
salt and freshly ground black pepper
leaves from 3 sprigs of thyme
chopped parsley to serve

Place all the ingredients except the parsley in an ovenproof baking dish. Mix and leave to marinate for 1 hour, stirring occasionally.

Preheat the oven to 200°C (400°F/Gas 6). Place the baking dish into the oven and cook for 45 minutes, basting once halfway through. (If the pan seems in danger of drying out when you baste the chicken, add a couple of tablespoons of water after basting.)

Check the meat is cooked through by piercing a piece to the bone. The juices should run clear and the meat should easily pull away from the bone. If not cooked, return to the oven for 5–10 minutes and check again. Allow it to rest, in the pan, for 5 minutes.

Serve the chicken and onions drizzled with a little of the pan juices, scatter over some parsley and finish with a squeeze of lemon juice.

LAMB KLEFTIKO

Legend has it that this dish came into being in the nineteenth century, when groups of revolutionaries hiding in the hills would cook meat (sometimes stolen) buried underground so that no smoke or steam would escape and give them away. You can make this with bone-in meat, but it will need a longer, slower cook. For a lighter version, omit the potatoes or cheese, but this is a great one-pot recipe if you do include them. You can also swap the lamb for pork.

SERVES 4

3 tablespoons olive oil, plus more to cook
600 g (1 lb 5 oz) boneless lamb shoulder, leg or shank, cut into bite-sized chunks
1 onion, finely sliced
6 garlic cloves
1 carrot, finely chopped
2 tomatoes, seeded and roughly chopped
2 large white potatoes, cut into chunks
80 g (3 oz/⅔ cup) hard goats' cheese or Greek manouri cheese, cut into small chunks
leaves from 1 sprig of rosemary
4 sprigs of thyme, broken into short lengths
juice of 1 lemon
1 teaspoon roughly chopped parsley leaves
salt and freshly ground black pepper

Preheat the oven to 180°C (350°F/Gas 4). Have ready a large metal roasting dish, on to which you've placed 2 long sheets of baking paper, crossed over to form an 'X' shape.

In a large wide pan, heat a little olive oil and brown the lamb all over, in batches so as not to crowd the pan. Remove from the pan and place in a bowl. Brown the onion over a high heat with a bit more oil in the same pan. Tip in with the lamb. Add all the other ingredients to the bowl (except the 3 tablespoons of olive oil), season generously and toss gently to ensure everything is coated and the herbs and cheese are well distributed.

Pour the whole lot on to the centre of the double layer of baking paper. Fold the edges upwards to ensure no liquid can escape and pour in the 3 tablespoons of olive oil and 3 tablespoons of water. Working with top layer of paper first, bring the two overhanging edges together and fold them in on themselves, using small folds, until you have folded down to the lamb. Then do the same with the second layer of paper, to form a really good seal so no steam can escape.

Cook for 1½ hours. Let the lamb rest in its parcel, out of the oven, for a further 15 minutes. Bring to the table still wrapped and open to release the cloud of fragrant steam at the table.

AUBERGINE BAKE WITH MEATBALLS & CHEESE

A hearty bake called *kikikeli*, meatballs tucked under aubergine (eggplant) and cheese, is perfect as a filling winter meal. To be extra authentic, if you can find Greek kasseri cheese, use 275g (10 oz) of that, replacing the mozzarella and the gruyère.

SERVES 4

AUBERGINE BAKE
1 aubergine (eggplant)
olive oil
salt
1 slice of white bread, crusts removed
3–4 tablespoons milk
1 onion
1 garlic clove
500 g (1 lb 2 oz/1¼ cups) minced (ground) beef
¼ teaspoon freshly ground black pepper
¼ teaspoon dried mint, or to taste
1 tablespoon finely chopped parsley leaves, or to taste
200 g (7 oz) buffalo mozzarella
75 g (2½ oz) gruyère

SAUCE
1 garlic clove, finely chopped
1 tablespoon tomato purée (paste)
1 tablespoon red wine vinegar
500 g (1 lb 2 oz/2 cups) passata (sieved tomatoes)
½ teaspoon dried Greek oregano

Preheat the oven to 200°C (400F/Gas 6).

Cut the aubergine into 5 mm (¼ in) slices. Brush a baking tray with olive oil and place the slices in a single layer on the tray. Brush the upper sides with oil, sprinkle over a little salt and place in the oven. Cook for about 15 minutes, turning once, or until soft and just beginning to brown. Set aside.

Meanwhile, prepare the meatballs. Shred the bread into small pieces and place in a bowl. Pour over enough milk to just cover. Soak for a couple of minutes, then lift out the bread and squeeze out the milk (discard the milk). Halve the onion and grate half of it, plus the garlic clove, into a bowl. Add the minced beef, soaked bread, ½ teaspoon of salt, the pepper and herbs.

Mix thoroughly with your hands, ensuring the herbs and onion are really well distributed.

Get a wide frying pan hot over a medium heat and add a splash of olive oil. Take a teaspoonful of the meat mixture and place in the pan. When cooked through, taste to check the seasoning and adjust it if necessary (you can also add more herbs if you like).

When you're happy with the seasoning, roll the rest of the meat mixture into 16–18 meatballs. Place in the pan and brown, turning regularly. Remove from the heat and set aside.

Make the tomato sauce: chop the remaining half onion finely and place in a pan with a little olive oil and a pinch of salt. Soften, but do not allow to brown, for about 10 minutes. Add the garlic and cook for 2 minutes. Add the tomato purée and cook, stirring, for 2 minutes, then add the vinegar and cook for a further minute. Finally add the passata and Greek oregano and season to taste. Cook for 5 minutes. Taste and adjust the seasoning if necessary.

Assemble the bake: Place the meatballs in a medium-sized baking dish, in a single layer. Rip one-quarter of the mozzarella into small pieces and tuck in between the meatballs. Pour over half the tomato sauce, then arrange over the aubergine slices. Pour on the rest of the sauce. Tear the remaining mozzarella into pieces and place over the sauce. Grate the gruyère on top.

Place in the oven and cook for 15–20 minutes, until the cheese has melted and is bubbling and golden.

Photograph overleaf

VEGETARIAN
MAINS & SIDES

VEGETABLES ARE TREATED
WITH JUST AS MUCH
RESPECT AS MEAT AND
FISH IN GREEK ISLAND
COOKING. TRADITIONAL
VEGETABLE DISHES ARE
OFTEN MADE WITH FORAGED
GREENS AND ARE ALWAYS
SEASONAL. THEY MAY LOOK
SIMPLE BUT LACED WITH
GARLIC, GOOD OLIVE OIL
OR TANGY CHEESES, THESE
VEGETARIAN DISHES ARE
FULL OF FLAVOUR. TRY EGGS
BAKED IN CREAMY STAKA,
SLOW ROASTED FENNEL OR
HEARTY LENTILS WITH CRISPY
ONIONS AND RICE.

AUBERGINES BAKED WITH FETA CHEESE

This is another deceptively simple dish. The combination of roasted aubergine (eggplant), garlic and feta, with a little olive oil, is perfect.

SERVES 2 as a main course or 4–6 as a starter

600 g (1 lb 5 oz) regular or baby aubergines (eggplants)
salt
1 garlic clove, finely chopped
4–5 tablespoons olive oil, plus more if needed
100–200 g (3½–7 oz/⅔–1⅓ cups) crumbled feta, depending on the size of the aubergines
chopped parsley leaves to serve

Preheat the oven to 200°C (400°F/Gas 6).

Cut the aubergines in half, then run a knife along the middle of the aubergine flesh lengthways, but not all the way through to the skin. Do the same, making a shorter cut, parallel to the central cut, on both sides. Lay them in a baking dish, cut side-up, and sprinkle with a pinch of salt. Press the garlic into the cuts and drizzle generously with the oil (use a little extra if they look dry). Finally, top each with some of the feta.

Bake in the oven for 15–25 minutes, depending on size. They are cooked when the aubergines are beginning to collapse and the cheese is just browning. Serve scattered with a little parsley.

CARAMELISED ONION & GOATS' BUTTER PASTA

This simple but tasty dish is traditional on several Greek islands, although some cooks like to add thick strained yoghurt to the sauce, or use sheeps' rather than goats' cheese, both of which are delicious. When a chef on Rhodes told me that the trick was to cook the onions with no fat at all, until they were 'red', I thought something had been lost in translation, but it does work (as long you keep stirring) and results in a very intense flavour. You can use regular butter if you prefer, but goats' butter is available in most large supermarkets.

SERVES 2

1 onion, finely sliced
pinch of fine salt
200 g (7 oz) dried spaghetti or linguine
generous knob of goats' butter
50 g (2 oz/½ cup) grated hard goats' cheese, or more to taste

Sprinkle the sliced onion with the salt, then cook over a very gentle heat, stirring very often, until they are a reddish-gold colour.

When the onion is ready, cook the pasta for 1 minute less than the packet instructions suggest. Drain, then return to the pan and add the butter, onion and half the cheese. Toss thoroughly.

Divide between 2 warmed bowls and serve with the rest of the cheese scattered on top.

BOUREKI, CHANIA STYLE

This is my version of a traditional dish of courgettes (zucchini), potatoes, cheese and herbs from Chania, Crete, a beautiful town with a Venetian harbour. It can be made with a filo pastry crust, but I prefer this slightly lighter version. You can easily make this wheat-free by leaving out the flour but this will result in a wetter dish, as the flour absorbs some of the liquid released by the courgettes as they cook.

SERVES 4 as a main course or 6–8 as a side dish

500 g (1 lb 2 oz) courgettes (zucchini), sliced about 3 mm (⅛ in) thick
500 g (1 lb 2 oz) potatoes, sliced about 3mm (⅛ in) thick
125 g (4 oz/1 cup) plain (all-purpose) flour
100 g (3½ oz/⅓ cup) ricotta
300 g (10½ oz/2 cups) mashed feta
90 ml (3 fl oz/⅓ cup) olive oil
½ teaspoon dried mint
2 teaspoon finely chopped mint leaves
2 garlic cloves, finely sliced
salt and freshly ground black pepper

Preheat the oven to 180°C (350°F/Gas 4).

Place the courgettes and potatoes in a large bowl and sprinkle over the flour, tossing to ensure all the slices get a light covering.

Mix together the cheeses and divide the mixture into 3. Divide the courgette mixture into 3 as well.

Pour about one-quarter of the oil into a large ovenproof baking dish and tilt it to completely coat the base. Arrange one-third of the courgette mixture in the dish, ensuring the entire base is covered and pressing the slices down firmly. Scatter over one-third of the cheese mixture. Add half the dried and fresh mint, with half the garlic. Drizzle over a third of the remaining oil and season generously with salt and freshly ground black pepper. Repeat the layering once more, pressing firmly on the slices so they are tightly packed in and drizzling with half the remaining oil. Repeat the layering for a final time, but without the herbs or garlic, which will have been used up.

Bake in the oven for 1 hour, checking every so often that the dish isn't drying out. If the top browns too fast, reduce the heat by 10°C (25°F/Gas 1) and cover with foil. Insert a skewer or sharp knife into the boureki to check the potatoes have cooked through. When they are tender, remove the dish from the oven and leave to stand for about 15 minutes, then serve warm.

VEGETARIAN MAINS & SIDES

FETA BAKED IN THE OVEN

Use ripe in-season peppers and tomatoes for this colourful dish, which makes a lovely vegetarian supper or quick sharing platter for a starter or meze, served with warm wholemeal bread or Flatbreads (page 32).

SERVES 2 as a main dish or 4 as a meze
olive oil for the dish
I large tomato, finely sliced
½ red or yellow (bell) pepper, finely sliced
pinch of salt
100 g (3½ oz) feta
pinch of sweet paprika
pinch of chilli flakes, or to taste

Preheat the oven to 200°C (400°F/Gas 6). Oil a baking dish.

Spread the sliced tomato and pepper out in the dish, toss in the oil and salt, and place in the oven for 5 minutes.

Remove from the oven and top with the feta cheese, broken into large chunks. Sprinkle with the paprika and chilli flakes and return to the oven. Bake for 15 minutes.

Serve immediately, drizzling over the pan juices before eating.

SLOW-COOKED FENNEL

I love the earthy, nutty quality that is brought out when you slow cook fennel. Fennel grows on many of the Greek islands, and the feathery fennel fronds are a crucial part of many dishes.

SERVES 2 as a side dish

I fennel bulb, quartered
2 knobs of butter
100 ml (3½ fl oz/scant ½ cup) white wine
leaves from 1 sprig of thyme
8 cherry tomatoes, halved
I garlic clove, peeled and left whole, but lightly bashed
salt and freshly ground pepper

Preheat the oven to 180°C (350°F/Gas 4) and put an ovenproof dish with a lid in the oven to heat up.

Cut off any particularly tough-looking parts at the base of the fennel. Place a frying pan over a medium heat and add a knob of butter. Brown the fennel gently for 5–6 minutes, turning to ensure as much of the surface browns as possible. When done, add another knob of butter to melt in the pan, then pour the fennel and butter into the hot baking dish.

Pour in the wine and add the thyme, tomatoes and bashed clove of garlic. Season lightly and return to the oven for 40 minutes. The fennel is cooked when it is very tender, and offers little resistance to the point of a knife.

Serve hot. You may like to discard the bashed garlic, pour off the sauce and reduce it slightly in a saucepan before pouring it back over the fennel.

SPICY GREENS

Chorta, wild Wilted Greens (page 192), are cooked on most islands, but this dish, *tsigarelli* is Corfu's spicy version, made with the addition of onion and chilli flakes or paprika. Any seasonal greens that wilt will work perfectly; try chard or beetroot greens when in season.

SERVES 4 as a side dish

2–3 tablespoons extra-virgin olive oil

1 small onion, finely sliced

salt

2 garlic cloves, crushed

½ fennel bulb, finely sliced (optional)

¼ teaspoon fennel seeds

1 head chicory (Belgian endive), leaves divided and sliced into bite-sized pieces, washed but not dried

100 g (3½ oz/2 packed cups) spinach, washed but not dried

100 g (3½ oz/3 packed cups) rocket (arugula), washed but not dried

2 spring onions (scallions), finely chopped

½ teaspoon chilli flakes, or to taste

½ teaspoon hot or sweet paprika

1 teaspoon lemon juice, or to taste

freshly ground black pepper

Place 1 tablespoon of the olive oil in a wide pan over a medium heat. Add the onion and a pinch of salt and cook for 6–8 minutes until just translucent. Add the garlic and fennel bulb, then the fennel seeds. Cook for 3–4 minutes, stirring and not allowing the contents of the pan to brown.

Add the wet leaves and spring onions, then stir in the spices. Reduce the heat to low and cover the pan. Leave to simmer gently for 2–3 minutes.

Add the lemon juice, 1–2 tablespoons of the remaining olive oil and some black pepper. Taste and decide if you'd like more lemon juice, salt or chilli flakes, and add more of each if necessary. Serve hot or at room temperature.

EGGS BAKED WITH STAKA CREAM

Staka is an incredibly rich creamy roux from Crete, made from staka goats' or sheeps' milk butter. The real thing is practically impossible to find outside Crete, but this is a good alternative. I like to eat this as part of a lazy brunch with hot toast, but it's often served as part of an evening meal with skinny fries or shards of crisp fried potato to dip in the yolks.

SERVES 2

40 g (1½ oz/⅓ stick) goats' butter, plus more for the dish
6 tablespoons double (heavy) cream
2 tablespoons grated pecorino
salt
2 eggs

Preheat the oven to 180°C (350°F/Gas 4). Butter 2 ramekins just large enough to take an egg and the sauce.

Melt the butter over a low heat. Remove from the heat and stir in the cream and pecorino. Taste to check it tastes cheesy rather than just of cream, and add more salt if the goats' butter isn't salty (but it often is). Pour a little sauce into each ramekin, then break in an egg. Top each with more of the sauce, so the eggs are barely visible. Place in the oven and bake for 8–10 minutes, depending on how firm you like your eggs. (Remember they will continue to firm up once out of the oven.)

Serve immediately.

LEMON, GARLIC & HERB ROASTED POTATOES

These potatoes make the kitchen smell wonderful as they roast.

SERVES 4

800 g (1 lb 12 oz) roasting potatoes, peeled and cut into 3 cm (1¼ in) chunks
1 whole head of garlic, cloves divided and peeled
juice of 1 lemon
1 teaspoon dried Greek oregano
½ teaspoon salt
½ teaspoon freshly ground black pepper
90 ml (3 fl oz/⅓ cup) olive oil
150 ml (5 fl oz/⅔ cup) chicken or vegetable stock

Preheat the oven to 200°C (400°F/Gas 6).

Place the potatoes and garlic in a large baking tray in a single layer (don't overcrowd the pan) and add the lemon juice, Greek oregano, salt, pepper and olive oil. Toss to ensure all the potatoes are well coated and the seasonings are evenly distributed. Pour the stock into the tray and place in the oven for 45 minutes. Keep an eye on the garlic as the cloves will cook quicker than the potatoes and, if they burn, they will taste bitter, so remove them and set aside once the garlic is golden brown.

After 45 minutes, turn the potatoes over, gently so they don't fall apart. Cook for another 10–15 minutes, or long enough for the undersides to crisp up. Turn once more to ensure a really golden colour all over the potatoes, return the garlic if you set it aside, then give them another 5 minutes in the oven.

Serve immediately.

SKORÐALIA

Skordalia is a very garlicky sauce that is often served alongside salt cod dishes (see photo, page 117). It can be made with bread, rather than potatoes as it is here, and sometimes doesn't contain almonds. The one constant though, is the garlic. My friend Gina, from Milos, recommends eating coffee grounds to get rid of the taste, and says it is a dish that either everyone at dinner must eat, or no one!

Don't be tempted to use a food processor or blender to mash the potato, as it will become gluey and inedible. A potato ricer is the best tool.

SERVES 4 as a side dish

500 g (1 lb 2 oz) floury potatoes
1 slice of day-old bread, crusts removed
a little milk
4 tablespoons extra-virgin olive oil
3 garlic cloves, mashed to a paste
2 tablespoons ground almonds (almond meal)
¼–½ teaspoon salt
1–2 teaspoons lemon juice

Peel the potatoes, cut into roughly equal chunks and cook in boiling water until soft; 15–20 minutes.

Meanwhile, soak the bread in a little milk. When it is soft, squeeze out the liquid and discard the milk.

Drain the potatoes and immediately mash really, really thoroughly (ideally using a ricer). Add the olive oil, soaked bread, garlic and ground almonds and mix vigorously until really smooth. Taste and add a little salt and a little lemon juice, gradually, until the taste is just right for you. It should be smooth and silky in texture with a strong garlic flavour.

Serve with salt cod dishes, as a dip on its own or with fried fish.

WILTED GREENS

This dish, *chorta*, is made with whatever greens are in season, sometimes foraged from the countryside or gathered at local markets.

SERVES 2 with other dishes

I tablespoon olive oil
I onion, finely chopped
I tomato, seeded and finely chopped
200 g (7 oz/6 packed cups) mixture of rocket, spinach, dandelion
(optional), fennel fronds
4 sprigs of parsley
I sprig of dill (dillweed), optional
extra-virgin olive oil
salt and freshly ground black pepper
I teaspoon lemon juice

Place the regular olive oil in a saucepan with a lid and it set over a low heat. Add the onion and cook, stirring regularly, until just translucent, about 10 minutes. Add the tomato and cook for a further 2 minutes.

Wash the leaves (including the herbs) thoroughly but don't dry them. Place the wet leaves in the pan. Put the lid on and steam the leaves. You can cook them for anything from just a couple of minutes for greens that are just wilted, or 10 minutes or more for *chorta* as you would find it on the islands, where they like their greens well cooked. Stir occasionally so the bottom leaves don't stick to the pan and to distribute the heat throughout.

When all the leaves have wilted, remove from the heat and drain. Dress with a little extra-virgin olive oil, salt and pepper and the lemon juice. Eat warm, lukewarm or cold.

COURGETTE FRITTATA

Courgette (zucchini), dill (dillweed) and mint elevate a simple omelette or frittata, known as *sfougato*, into something much more special, studded with little nuggets of melted cheese.

If you don't have a small ovenproof frying pan, tip the mixture from the frying pan into a small 500 ml (17 fl oz/2¼ cup) oven dish, and cook it in that.

SERVES 2 as a light meal or 4 as part of a meze
1 tablespoon olive oil
½ small onion, finely chopped
salt and freshly ground black pepper
1 courgette (zucchini), about 200g (7 oz), coarsely grated
4 eggs
1–2 tablespoons single (light) cream or milk (optional)
1 spring onion (scallion), finely chopped
1 tablespoon finely chopped dill (dillweed)
1 teaspoon finely chopped mint leaves
25 g (1 oz) feta, or mild goats' or sheeps' cheese

Preheat the oven to 180°C (350°F/Gas 4).

Put the oil in a small ovenproof frying pan, if you have one, and warm over a medium-low heat. Add the onion and a pinch of salt and cook for 2 minutes. Next, add the courgette and cook for about 10 minutes, until the courgette has softened and most of the liquid has evaporated away. Don't allow to brown. Remove from the heat.

Whisk together the eggs and cream or milk. Add the spring onion and herbs and season generously with salt and pepper.

Pour the egg mixture over the courgettes and stir gently to combine. Crumble the cheese over the top. Place the pan on the middle shelf of the oven. Cook for 20–25 minutes, until risen slightly from the pan and lightly golden on top.

Remove from the oven and leave to cool a little in the pan. Serve warm or at room temperature.

GREEK VEGETABLE BAKE

By cooking layers of Mediterranean vegetables together with plenty of olive oil, they become much more than the sum of their parts. This dish is called *briam*.

SERVES 2 as a main course

5 tablespoons olive oil
175 g (6 oz) potato, in 1 cm (½ in) slices
1 onion, sliced into fine semi-circles
1 courgette (zucchini), about 200 g (7 oz), in 5 mm (¼ in) slices
1 (bell) pepper in 1 cm (½ in) strips
½ aubergine (eggplant), in 5 mm (¼ in) slices
2 tomatoes in 5 cm (¼ in) slices
2 tablespoons finely chopped parsley leaves
salt and freshly ground black pepper
½ teaspoon tomato purée (paste)

Preheat the oven to 180°C (350°F/Gas 4).

In a large, wide sauté pan, heat 3 tablespoons of the olive oil over a medium-high heat. Add the potato, onion, courgette, pepper and aubergine and sauté for 5 minutes, stirring often, just enough to get a little colour on the vegetables. Remove from the heat.

Using tongs, remove the potato and place in a layer on the bottom of a 1 litre (34 fl oz/4¼ cup) ovenproof dish. Follow with a layer of courgette, picking up some of the onion as you go. Next add the aubergine and then the pepper, along with more onion. Alternatively, just layer up the vegetables as you prefer. Finish with the tomatoes and parsley and season generously with salt and pepper.

Whisk the tomato purée into 150 ml (5 fl oz/⅔ cup) of water to dissolve, then pour over the dish. Finish by drizzling with the final 2 tablespoons of olive oil.

Place in the oven and cook for 30 minutes, then remove and baste the vegetables with the juices. Reduce the oven temperature to 160°C (325°F/Gas 3) and cook for a further 1 hour, checking every 20 minutes or so that the liquid hasn't got too low, and that the vegetables aren't browning too fast. Top up with a little more water, or cover with foil, if necessary.

Remove from the oven when the vegetables are just charred on the top and meltingly soft all the way through. Leave to stand for 10–15 minutes before serving, with plenty of good bread to mop up the juices.

RICE WITH LENTILS & CRISPY ONIONS

Fakorizo is a great vegetarian main course. By adding more water, you can make it into a soup; by adding more rice you can turn it into a pilaf and serve as a hearty side, perhaps with some lamb chops or barbecued chicken. In Cyprus, a similar dish is called *moukentra*, and is served with fresh coriander (cilantro) and chilli flakes.

Don't add salt or lemon juice until the lentils are cooked, otherwise they may not soften, and be sure not to use tomato purée with added salt, for the same reason.

SERVES 2 as a main course, or 4 as a side dish
100 g (3½ oz/½ cup) green or brown lentils
60 g (2 oz/⅓ cup) long-grain white rice
1 large onion, finely sliced
a little olive oil
1 teaspoon tomato purée (paste)
salt and freshly ground black pepper
lemon juice to taste to serve
Greek yoghurt or feta cheese to serve (optional)
finely chopped mint or parsley leaves to serve (optional)

Check the packet to see if your lentils require soaking overnight and rinsing. Many types of green lentils do not, but if yours do, follow the directions. When ready to cook, soak the rice in cold water for 20 minutes, drain, then rinse twice in fresh water.

In a non-reactive (non-aluminium) saucepan, gently cook the onion in oil over a medium heat for 15 minutes (without salt) until deep golden brown. Stir often to ensure it doesn't burn. Remove half the onion and set aside. Add the tomato purée to the pan and cook, stirring, for 3 minutes. Add the lentils to the pan with enough hot water to just cover them. Bring to a gentle simmer and cook for 20–40 minutes, depending on the type of lentils you are using. Stir occasionally and add a little more water if necessary.

When the lentils are tender, add the rice and a few more tablespoonfuls of water if the pan is too dry, and cook the rice for 10 minutes or until tender, stirring occasionally (soaking the rice will allow it cook faster). Season to taste with salt and pepper and a squeeze of lemon juice.

Serve scattered with the reserved onions (reheat them if necessary), adding a spoonful of yoghurt or some crumbled feta or fresh herbs, if you like.

DESSERTS,
SWEETS
& DRINKS

IN ALMOST EVERY RESTAURANT ON THE ISLANDS, YOU WILL ALWAYS BE GIVEN SOMETHING SMALL AND SWEET BEFORE YOU CAN LEAVE. IT MIGHT BE A SPOON SWEET, PRESERVED FRUIT SERVED ON A TINY SPOON WITH A GLASS OF WATER; A WARM LITTLE LOUKOUMADES DOUGHNUT OR TWO, DUSTED IN SUGAR AND SESAME SEEDS; A SQUARE OF ORANGE-SCENTED CUSTARD TART OR A SYRUP-DRENCHED CAKE.

GALAKTOBOUREKO

I learned to make this one scorching afternoon on the bougainvillea-draped terrace of a hotel called the Lindian Village on Rhodes. The pastry chef had offered to teach us a few local dishes, and this beautiful, orange-scented custard dessert was one of them. He also let us in on his secret baking ingredient: love. 'With love, everything becomes tasty and beautiful,' he said.

MAKES 12 generous pieces

GALAKTOBOUREKO
1 litre (34 fl oz/4¼ cups) milk
60 g (2 oz/½ cup) semolina (semolina flour)
125 g (4 oz/generous ½ cup) caster (superfine) sugar
5 eggs
finely grated zest of ½ orange
1 teaspoon vanilla extract or vanilla bean paste
70 g (2¼ oz/⅔ stick) unsalted butter, melted, plus more for the dish
250 g (10 oz) filo pastry

SYRUP
100 g (3½ oz/scant ½ cup) caster (superfine) sugar
2 cloves
finely grated zest ½ orange and the juice of 1 orange
finely grated zest of ½ unwaxed lemon

Start with the galaktoboureko. Heat 750 ml (25 fl oz/3 cups) of the milk and add the semolina and sugar. Stir often and bring slowly to the boil, then reduce the heat and simmer for 10 minutes. Meanwhile, whisk the remaining cold milk with the eggs until well combined. Slowly add a ladleful of the hot semolina mixture to the egg mixture and whisk thoroughly. (This is to help the temper the eggs to the heat so they won't cook and curdle.) Slowly and steadily, whisking continuously, pour the cold egg and milk mixture into the hot milk and semolina mixture. Cook gently, stirring all the time, until the custard begins to thicken. Remove from the heat. Add the orange zest and vanilla extract or paste and leave to cool.

Preheat the oven to 180°C (350°F/Gas 4). Butter a deep 20 cm (8 in) square or rectangular baking dish. Lay a sheet of pastry so that half of it sits snugly in the dish and the other half hangs over the end, and brush with melted butter. Do the same at the opposite end of the dish, then at both the other sides, brushing each layer with butter. Cut 2 sheets of pastry in half and arrange so they cover the base and reach up the sides, covering the joins in each corner, and brush them with butter. Pour the cooled custard carefully into the dish.

Starting with the last piece of pastry you laid down, gently lift the overhanging half up and lie it over the custard, as flat as possible. Brush it with butter. Then pull over the next piece and continue, buttering each layer as you fold. Finally

cut 2 pieces of pastry to fit inside the top of the dish. Lay them on top of the other pastry layers and butter each one.

Very gently score portion marks on top of the prepared dish, so it's easier to cut up later. (If you have time, it's easier to do this if you pop the dish into the freezer for 15 minutes.)

Bake for 50 minutes, or until the top is golden brown and crispy. Allow to cool.

Make the syrup: place the sugar, cloves, orange and lemon zests and orange juice in a pan, pour in 100 ml (3½ fl oz/scant ½ cup) of water and bring to a boil. Stir to ensure the sugar has dissolved, reduce the heat and simmer for 15 minutes. Strain the syrup.

Once the galaktoboureko has cooled, pour the hot syrup over the dish; you may not need all of it, so pour slowly. Leave to stand for 30 minutes before serving. The syrup will soak into the lower layers of the pudding which will be deliciously sweet, while the top will be crisp and crunchy, with the wobbly, orange-scented custard in between.

FIGS POACHED IN WINE

Olive, pomegranate and fig trees dot the Greek islands. In season the figs are lusciously sweet. Away from the islands it can be hard to find perfectly ripe figs, so I like to poach them in spiced wine. The first time I tried this, the figs were poached in vinsanto, a glorious amber-coloured sweet wine made in Santorini from sun-dried grapes, but back home it is both expensive and hard to find, so I use a mixture of dessert wine and red wine to replicate the flavour.

SERVES 6
400 ml (13 fl oz/1¾ cups) sweet or dessert wine
200 ml (7 fl oz/scant 1 cup) red wine
125 g (4 oz/½ cup) caster (superfine) sugar
1 cinnamon stick
6 cloves
12 fresh figs, halved
Greek yoghurt to serve

Place both wines, the sugar, cinnamon and cloves in a pan and bring to the boil, stirring to ensure the sugar dissolves. Boil hard for 2 minutes; be careful not to allow the liquid to boil over.

Prick each fig a few times with a pin to ensure the syrup penetrates them as they cook. Reduce the heat to its lowest and place the figs into the wine mixture. Cover and simmer for 3 minutes, adding 1–2 minutes more if you prefer your figs soft or if they are very under-ripe. (Taste a fig after 3 minutes and decide if you'd like to cook it for longer.) Remove the figs from the pan and set aside.

Increase the heat under the syrup and, with the lid off, bring back to a rolling boil. Cook until reduced by half. Serve with the figs either warm or cold, with the syrup and a dollop of Greek yoghurt on the side.

GRAPE SPOON SWEETS

Spoon sweets, *stafili gliko*, fruits or occasionally nuts preserved in syrup, are often served alongside the bill at the end of a meal in a Greek restaurant or as a treat if you are a guest in someone's home. They are called spoon sweets because they are served on a tiny spoon, alongside a glass of water. They are also good with yoghurt, on hot buttered toast or even with strong cheese. Many of the islands have their own special spoon sweets: on Chios, a white spoon sweet is made from the island's famous resin, mastic, while on Ikaria sour cherries or walnuts are used. Naxos' speciality is quince and Santorini's is made from almonds. This is a slightly simplified version of the traditional recipe.

MAKES ABOUT 800 g (1 lb 12 oz) preserve
500 g (1 lb 2 oz/2 cups) caster (superfine) sugar
juice of ½ lemon
500 g (1 lb 2 oz/2⅔ cups) seedless grapes

Sterilise enough tempered glass jam jars to comfortably fit about 800 g (1 lb 12 oz) grape preserve, by rinsing in boiling water or placing in a low oven for 15 minutes.

Place the sugar and lemon juice in a large non-reactive pan, pour in 250 ml (8½ fl oz/1 cup) water and bring to the boil. As it comes to the boil, stir gently to ensure all the sugar is dissolved, otherwise small crystals will remain in the syrup.

Boil until the syrup reaches 110°C (225°F) on a jam thermometer, which will take anywhere from 10–20 minutes. Keep an eye on the pan and stir frequently to prevent it boiling over. (To check if the preserve has reached setting point without a thermometer, place a saucer in the freezer. When the mixture has been boiling for 5 minutes or so, drop a tiny bit of the syrup on the saucer. Leave for 30 seconds, then tilt the saucer. If the syrup runs straight across the surface, setting point hasn't been reached. If it doesn't run, the preserve has set.)

Continue to boil for 5 minutes. Don't let it get too hot or the sugar in the jam will reach candy setting point, which will make it very hard to get out of the pan or jars.

Place the fruit into the syrup mixture and simmer for 15 minutes. Allow to cool slightly and pour into the sterilised jam jars. Seal the tops with wax paper to prevent mould forming, then secure the lids. Keep in a cool, dark place for up to 2 months.

ALMOND COOKIES

These little almond cookies, *amygdalota*, are from Mykonos and are lovely with a cup of strong Greek coffee.

MAKES 20

butter, for the baking tray
2 egg whites, beaten until white and fluffy
250 g (8 oz/2½ cups) ground almonds (almond meal)
200 g (7 oz/scant 1 cup) caster (superfine) sugar
½ teaspoon orange flower extract (optional)
icing sugar to serve

Preheat the oven to 180°C (350°F/Gas 4).

Line a baking tray with buttered baking paper. In a bowl, mix the beaten egg whites, ground almonds, sugar and orange flower extract (if using) and stir well.

Scoop up tablespoons of the mixture and roll into 20 balls. Place on the baking paper and press down lightly, to form a round cookie shape.

Bake in the oven for 20 minutes or until golden brown, crisp on the outside and just squidgy in the middle, turning the tray round for the last 5 minutes to ensure a really even golden colour all over. Dust with icing sugar to serve.

VARIATION: try this vegan version of *amygdalota*.

250 g (8 oz/2½ cups) ground almonds (almond meal)
200 g (7 oz/scant 1 cup) caster (superfine) sugar
½ teaspoon orange flower extract or rose water (optional)
icing sugar to serve

Mix the almonds, sugar and orange flower extract or rose water (if using) with 90 ml (3 fl oz/⅓ cup) of water. Place in a saucepan and heat gently until the sugar has dissolved. (It will be quite dry, but don't panic.) Check whether the grittiness of the sugar has disappeared by carefully tasting a little of the hot mix and cook gently for a little longer if necessary. Remove from the heat and leave just until cool enough to handle. (However, don't leave the mixture too long as it sets quickly, making it harder to shape and even harder to wash off the pan.)

Traditionally this is served in small pear-shaped pieces, with cloves to look like stalks, but I prefer little balls: form them to about the size of marbles with the palms of your hands and place on a plate. Dust with icing sugar. Leave to firm up, then place in a sealed box until ready to serve, to prevent drying out.

CRETAN HERB TEA

I was first served this fragrant tea at a women's co-operative on Crete, where women come together to cook and sell local traditional foodstuffs, as well as teach visitors how to make them.

SERVES 1

4 sprigs of thyme
4 sprigs of rosemary
4 or 5 sage leaves
1 teaspoon clear honey or grape syrup, or to taste

Clap each of the herb sprigs or leaves firmly between your hands to help release the aromatic oils. Place in a teapot.

Bring 200 ml (7 fl oz/scant 1 cup) of water to the boil, then leave it to stand for 2 minutes. Pour it into the teapot and leave to stand for 3–4 minutes.

Strain into a cup and add honey or grape syrup to taste.

TIGANITES

I was taught how to make these eggless fritters at a pretty seaside restaurant called Perigiali at Stegna beach on Rhodes. They are lovely for breakfast or as an easy dessert.

SERVES 4
100 g (3½ oz/¾ cup) '00' flour
100 ml (3½ fl oz/scant ½ cup) milk
juice of 1 squeezed orange, plus the finely grated zest of 2 oranges
generous pinch of salt
vegetable oil to fry
honey to serve
cinnamon to dust

Mix the flour and milk together with a whisk, then gradually add the orange juice and half the zest, continuing to whisk to avoid lumps. Finally add the salt. Leave the batter to stand for 10 minutes.

Pour oil into a wide frying pan to a depth of about 2 cm (¾ in). Pour a third of a ladleful of the batter into the hot oil, then repeat to make 3–4 fritters (do not crowd the pan). Cook for a minute, carefully turning in the oil once to ensure both sides turn golden brown. When a deep gold in colour, remove from the oil and drain on paper towels.

Serve immediately, drizzled with honey, scattered with a little of the remaining orange zest and dusted with cinnamon, while you cook the rest.

POMEGRANATE & GREEK YOGHURT PANNA COTTA

This is easy to make but impressive to serve, with the white panna cotta drizzled with bright red syrup and tiny pomegranate seeds. The syrup is very sweet, so don't add too much sugar to the pannacotta.

MAKES 6 (or 8 if you use small ramekins)

PANNA COTTA
5 gelatine leaves
250 ml (8½ fl oz/1 cup) milk
400 g (14 oz/1⅔ cups) Greek yoghurt
150 ml (5 fl oz/⅔ cup) double (heavy) cream
finely grated zest of ½ orange (optional)
1½ tablespoons caster (superfine) sugar

SYRUP
150 ml (5 fl oz/⅔ cup) pomegranate juice
3 tablespoons caster (superfine) sugar
finely grated zest and juice of ½ orange
pomegranate seeds to serve

Separate the gelatine leaves and place in cold water to soak for 5 minutes.

Meanwhile, in a pan over a low heat, warm the milk, yoghurt, cream, orange zest and sugar, stirring constantly. Don't allow to boil. Once hot, remove from the heat. Squeeze out excess liquid from the soaked gelatine, add it to the pan and stir to dissolve. Once fully dissolved, pour into 6–8 jelly moulds, ramekins or even cocktail glasses. Cover with plastic wrap and place in the fridge to set for at least 5 hours and preferably overnight.

Well in advance of serving, make the syrup: if you pour hot syrup over the panna cottas, they will melt, so you need to leave time for the syrup to cool. Place all the ingredients except the pomegranate seeds into a non-reactive (non-aluminium) pan and bring to the boil. Simmer until reduced by half to three-quarters and thick enough to just coat the back of a spoon. (It will foam up, so keep an eye on it to avoid it boiling over.) Cool and strain out the zest.

To un-mould the puddings, pour 3 cm (1¼ in) of hot water into a wide shallow bowl. Dip the panna cotta moulds briefly into the water for no longer than 5 seconds, being careful not to get water on the puddings themselves. Turn out on to serving plates, drizzle with a spoonful of the cooled syrup and scatter with pomegranate seeds.

LEMØN & BASIL GRANITA

Basil is considered a sacred plant across much of Greece and many churches are surrounded by dozens of beautifully scented basil bushes. It's also used decoratively, and you often find a little tub of it growing on café tables. The combination of lemon and basil takes me straight back to sunny afternoons exploring turquoise-and-white-painted hilltop villages.

You can make this with shop-bought still lemonade, as long as it's of good quality, but making your own is even better. Obviously, if you're making this for children, omit the vodka.

LEMONADE
pared zest and juice of 5 unwaxed lemons
150 g (5 oz/¾ cup) caster (superfine) sugar

GRANITA
2 tablespoons basil leaves, or to taste
finely grated zest of ½ unwaxed lemon
300 ml (10 fl oz/1¼ cups) still lemonade
2 teaspoons vodka (optional)

To make the lemonade, put the zest, juice and sugar in a large saucepan, pour in 350 ml (12 fl oz/1⅓ cups) of water and slowly bring to the boil. Simmer for 1–2 minutes and stir to ensure the sugar dissolves. Remove from the heat, strain, and allow to cool. (To drink your lemonade, dilute 2 parts of lemonade with 3 parts of water.)

For the granita, tear the basil leaves into pieces, then pound in a mortar and pestle. Add them and the lemon zest to the lemonade and mix well. Taste and add more basil or zest, if you like. Add the vodka (if using).

Pour into a sealable plastic box and cover with a lid. Put into the freezer for 2 hours, then remove and rough up with a fork to break up the ice crystals. Cover and return to the freezer.

When ready to serve, scrape the surface with a fork again to rough up the crystals (the vodka will help prevent it from freezing solid). Serve in sundae glasses or cocktail glasses.

FROZEN GREEK YOGHURT WITH BERRIES

This simple but creamy frozen yoghurt dessert can be made without an ice cream machine.

SERVES 2
500 g (1 lb 2 oz/2 cups) Greek yoghurt
caster (superfine) sugar
100 g (3½ oz/scant 1 cup) fresh or frozen berries

Line a sieve with muslin or paper towels and pour in the yoghurt. Set aside to drain for a couple of hours. Discard the liquid.

Once the yoghurt has drained and thickened, beat in 2 teaspoons of sugar with a whisk. Pour into a plastic tub or bowl and cover with a lid or plastic wrap. Place in the freezer. After 1 hour, remove from the freezer and stir vigorously with a fork. Repeat the freezing and the stirring twice. If you need to leave it for longer (or accidentally forget about it!), break the frozen yoghurt into chunks, place in the food processor and blitz until smooth again. Return to the freezer for 5 minutes before serving.

Meanwhile, prepare the berries. Place in a pan with 2 more tablespoons of sugar over a medium heat and cook until just beginning to fall apart and release their juice. Taste and add more sugar, if necessary. Cool.

Serve the frozen yoghurt with the fruit spooned over.

SESAME SWEETS

I spent a lovely morning at a women's co-operative in Apollonia, a hill town in Rhodes, learning make *pasteli* sesame sweets, or *melekouni* as those from Rhodes are called, by boiling honey, mixing it with seseame and spices and then hammering it flat with my hands. *Pasteli* are eaten at celebratory occasions, especially weddings, and the small kitchen produces almond-studded sweets that are brought by natives of Rhodes getting married all over the world. The women, who are all from Apollonia, told me about the traditions that accompany weddings: if you are single you should place your *melekouni* under your pillow and you'll dream of the man you will marry. The bride might also write the names of her single friends on the soles of her shoes; those that are rubbed off by her dancing will be married next.

This recipe is much easier to make if you have a sugar thermometer; they are reasonably cheap and easy to come by.

MAKES ABOUT 15–20 pieces
200 g (7 oz/1⅓ cups) raw sesame seeds
15–20 blanched almonds
200 g (7 oz/generous ½ cup) clear honey
50 g (2 oz/¼ cup) caster (superfine) sugar
⅛ teaspoon ground cinnamon
⅛ teaspoon ground nutmeg
1 teaspoon vegetable or other flavourless cooking oil, or more if needed

Preheat the the oven to 180°C (350°F/Gas 4).

Pour the sesame seeds into a baking tray and place the tray in the oven for 15 minutes, or until golden all over. Place the almonds in a separate tray and roast for 10 minutes, until golden all over.

Place the honey into a high-sided pan and add the sugar. Bring to the boil and boil until you reach 127°C (260°F). This is known as hard ball temperature; without reaching it, the sesame sweets won't set. Watch like a hawk to ensure it doesn't boil over, and stir it carefully to help ensure it doesn't.

Remove from the heat and add the spices. Next, stir in the sesame seeds. The mix should be firm and fairly hard to stir. Grease a baking tray with the oil.

Pour the hot honey and sesame mix onto the tray. Using a wooden spoon to start with, push the mixture out so that it begins to flatten over the tray. When cool enough, it is far easier to do this with your hands (but don't burn yourself). Once evenly distributed over the bottom of the tray, you need to make it denser, so that it is quite strong when set. Start in one corner, and working methodically tap firmly the surface with the palm of one hand. You will see the mix become firmer as the seeds are pressed together and the surface will become smoother. Then press with your fingers to make it even smoother. The mixture should be about 3 mm (¼ in) thick. Use a knife to mark diamonds on the

surface, pressing almost all the way through. Stud the top of each sweet with an almond.

Leave overnight to set, then break into diamond-shaped pieces. The sweets will keep for months in a sealed container.

WATERMELON PIE

Another wonderful example of island cooks making the best of the ingredients around them, this is a very old recipe from Milos. It is a really unusual tart that – quite honestly – will look as though it's never going to work, but will come out of the oven magically transformed into a beautiful deep pink dessert. This is another recipe from Vasiliki Drounga, who owns Paleos, a cake and pastry shop in Plaka, on Milos.

SERVES 6–8

125 g (4 oz/½ cup) caster (superfine) sugar
150 g (5 oz/1¼ cups) plain (all-purpose) flour, plus more to dust
850 g (1 lb 14 oz) watermelon, skin and seeds removed and cut into chestnut-sized pieces
90 ml (3 fl oz/⅓ cup) olive oil
1 tablespoon raw sesame seeds
½ teaspoon ground cinnamon to serve
clear honey to serve

Preheat the oven to 200°C (400°F/Gas 6). Have ready a non-stick cake tin, ideally 30 cm (12 in) round with sides at least 4 cm (1½ in) high and with a fixed base (this recipe contains a lot of liquid which will run out if you use a tin with a loose base).

In a large bowl, mix the sugar and flour together. Then add the watermelon pieces and gently stir to mix, but not too much or the watermelon will fall apart. You should have a loose, pale pink batter full of chunks of watermelon. It will look like pink scrambled eggs and you will never believe it will work at this stage! Keep the faith; it will.

Pour the oil into the cake tin and tilt it to ensure the entire base and sides are covered, then pour the watermelon mix on top. Spread it out, gently, so that it lies in an even layer across the tin. Scatter the sesame seeds over the top and place in the hot oven. Bake for 1–1½ hours, or until the batter has turned golden brown on top, is brown on the bottom and the edges are pulling away from the sides of the pan. Remove from the oven and cool in the tin, then use a spatula to gently lift it out of the tin. Serve warm, dusted with cinnamon and drizzled with a little honey.

GREEK DOUGHNUTS

These *loukoumades* are sweet little street food snacks, often sold harbour-side or at ports around Greece. They are dangerously easy to make and very moreish.

Once you've mastered these, try studding the centre with a little nugget of dark chocolate before frying.

MAKES ABOUT 28 small doughnuts
I tablespoon dry active yeast
200 ml (7 fl oz/scant I cup) lukewarm water
50 g (2 oz/¼ cup) caster (superfine) sugar, plus more to dust (optional)
2 tablespoons Greek yoghurt
250 g (9 oz/2 cups) plain (all-purpose) flour
¼ teaspoon baking powder
½ teaspoon fine salt
vegetable oil for frying
clear honey to coat (optional)
2 tablespoons walnuts, crumbled, or 2 teaspoons sesame seeds, toasted

Mix the yeast and half the water together with I teaspoon of the sugar. Leave for 10 minutes to become frothy. Add the yoghurt to the yeast mixture and whisk together.

In a bowl, mix the flour, the remaining sugar, baking powder and salt together. Whisk in the yeast mixture, plus gradually add the remaining water, to make a thick batter (you may not need it all). Cover and leave to rise somewhere warm for I hour.

Pour about 5 cm (2 in) of vegetable oil into a high-sided saucepan and place over a moderate heat. Using a pan thermometer, heat the oil to 180°C (350°F), or when a cube of day-old bread sizzles and browns in 30 seconds.

Have ready a small spoon in a glass of water. To shape the doughnuts, plunge your hand into the doughnut batter, and get a little of the mix into the palm of your hand. Over the bowl and with your thumb facing upwards, slowly clench your fist. You will see a little blob of the batter rising out of the hole formed by your fingers and thumb. When it is about the size of a marble, take the wet spoon in your other hand, scoop off the blob and place in the hot oil. Do this carefully as the water on the spoon will make the oil spit. Try not to use more than a marble-sized amount of batter, otherwise the dough may not cook through properly. Cook 4–5 at a time, being careful not to overcrowd the pan. Allow the *loukoumades* to cook for about 2½ minutes, or until they are golden brown, turning if necessary. If the oil is too hot, they will brown very fast but remain uncooked in the middle, so you may need to do a few experi-

Any excuse is a good excuse to order a powerful Greek coffee and a little plate of something sweet.

mental *loukoumades* and break them open to see if they are cooked within as well.

Remove from the pan with a slotted spoon and drain on paper towels, while you continue to cook the rest. Roll in a little sugar or drizzle with honey. Scatter with crumbled walnuts or sesame seeds to serve. Eat while warm.

OLIVE OIL COOKIES

These vegan crunchy, spiced cookies make a good mid-morning treat.

MAKES 16 cookies

250 g (9 oz/2 cups) plain (all-purpose) flour
1 teaspoon baking powder
100 g (3½ oz/scant ½ cup) caster (superfine) sugar
½ teaspoon ground cinnamon
½ teaspoon ground cloves
finely grated zest and juice of ½ unwaxed lemon
finely grated zest and juice of ½ small orange
90 ml (3 fl oz/⅓ cup) olive oil
1 tablespoon brandy (optional)
40 g (1½ oz/⅓ cup) sesame seeds

Preheat the oven to 180°C (350°F/Gas 4).

Stir together all the dry ingredients (except the sesame seeds) with the zests. Mix the liquids together and add to the dry ingredients. Stir until a firm dough is formed. If it seems too dry and crumbly, add 1–2 tablespoons of water.

Using your hands, shape the dough into a firm ball. Pull marble-sized pieces of dough from the ball and roll into sausage shapes about 10 cm (4 in) long, then pull the ends together to form a ring. Wet the ends to ensure they stick together. Do this with all the dough.

Pour the sesame seeds on to a plate. Mist or brush each ring with water. Gently roll the rings in the sesame seeds so they are coated all over, transfer to a baking sheet and place in the oven. Cook for 15 minutes, until golden brown all over. Transfer to a wire rack to cool. Store in an airtight container.

WALNUT BAKLAVA RØLLS

Baklava rolls are notoriously tricky to make, but this is a much simpler way. Many of the islands don't have pistachio trees, so baklava are made with local nuts instead, in this case, walnuts. Sheets of filo come in various sizes, so you may need to use 4 smaller sheets and not cut them in half. They're delicious served with strong Greek coffee.

MAKES ABOUT 20 pieces

ROLLS
125 g (4 oz/1 stick) unsalted butter, melted
200 g (7 oz/2 cups) walnut pieces
3 tablespoons caster (superfine) sugar
2 large sheets of filo pastry

SYRUP
100 g (3½ oz/½ cup) caster (superfine) sugar
juice of ½ lemon

Preheat the oven to 170°C (340°F/Gas 3½). Grease a baking tray with a little of the butter.

Start with the rolls. Using a mortar and pestle, roughly crush the walnut pieces. (Alternatively place in a sandwich bag and bash with a rolling pin.) Add the sugar.

Lay a sheet of filo out on a work surface and cut into 2 rectangles each measuring about 30 × 20 cm (12 × 8 in). Brush with melted butter. Scatter about a quarter of the walnuts evenly over the filo. Working from a short edge, begin to roll up the filo like a Swiss roll. Brush with butter every time you expose unbuttered pastry. Continue until you run out of pastry.

Transfer the filled roll of pastry to the prepared tray. Continue rolling and buttering more pastry and nuts until you have run out of nuts. Using a sharp knife, slice each roll of pastry into 5–6 evenly sized pieces.

Place in the oven and cook for 20 minutes, until golden brown all over and crisp.

Meanwhile make the syrup. Pour 120 ml (4 fl oz/½ cup) of water into a saucepan and add the sugar and lemon juice. Bring to the boil and boil for 10 minutes, reducing the volume by about a quarter. Remove the pastries from the oven and place in a single layer in a shallow dish, then pour over the syrup. Leave for 30 minutes or so for the syrup to soak into the pastry.

Serve with strong Greek coffee.

SWEET EASTER BREAD

This brioche-like bread, *tsoureki*, is usually made for Easter. Like brioche, it's lovely at breakfast-time. Other versions contain raisins, orange zest, fennel seeds or even chocolate chips, mixed into the dough before it rises. For a truly authentic *tsoureki*, add a pinch of ground *mahlep*: almond-flavoured ground sour cherry stones (pits).

MAKES 2 loaves
140 ml (4½ fl oz/scant ⅔ cup) milk
1 tablespoon dry active yeast
75 g (2½ oz/⅓ cup) caster (superfine) sugar
500 g (1 lb 2 oz/4 cups) strong white (bread) flour
½ teaspoon fine salt
150 g (5 oz/1¼ sticks) unsalted butter, melted and cooled
2 eggs, lightly beaten, plus 1 egg yolk to brush
1 teaspoon flavourless vegetable oil, for the tray
3 tablespoons flaked almonds

Warm the milk very gently until just lukewarm. Whisk in the yeast and 1 tablespoon of the sugar. Set aside for 10 minutes to become frothy.

Sift the flour into a large bowl and add the salt and remaining sugar. Whisk the melted butter and the two beaten eggs together, then whisk into the yeast and milk mixture. Make a well in the flour mixture and pour in the liquid. Stir to combine, using your hands as the dough begins to come together. Knead, using your hands or a dough hook attached to a mixer, for about 5 minutes, until the dough is smooth and pliable. Cover the dough with plastic wrap and leave somewhere warm for 1–1½ hours or so, to rise and double in size.

Oil a large baking tray.

To shape the breads, knock back the dough to more or less its original size. Divide into 6. Shape each piece into a long rope about 2 cm (¾ in) across and 30 cm (12 in) long. Lie 3 pieces next to each and pinch the ends together, wetting the ends to help them stick. Then gently plait the ropes of dough together. When you reach the end of the ropes, tuck the ends under neatly. Repeat with the other 3 ropes. You will now have 2 plaited loaves. Place on the prepared baking tray, cover with plastic wrap and place somewhere warm for 20 minutes to rise again.

When ready to bake, preheat the oven to 190°C (375°F/Gas 5).

Whisk the egg yolk with 1 teaspoon of water. Brush each loaf with the egg wash and scatter over the almonds. Bake in the oven for 20 minutes, until risen and golden all over. If the top is browning too fast after 10 minutes, reduce

the oven temperature by 10°C (25°F/Gas 1) or so and keep an eye on it for the remainder of the cooking time.

Remove from the oven and transfer to a wire rack to cool. Don't break into the bread when it is still hot, tempting as that may be, as much of the moisture will escape if you do, which can make the bread dry.

SEMOLINA CAKE

This is a little like the famous eastern Mediterranean *revani* cake but is also similar to *amygdolopita*, a Greek almond cake. It is quite a thin cake, so don't be alarmed it it doesn't rise much. It makes a lighter sweet treat as it is, but if you want something deeper, make two cakes, and sandwich them together with jam or lemon butter icing. (For a recipe for *revani*, see my previous book, *Istanbul: Recipes from the heart of Turkey*)

MAKES I cake

CAKE
butter, for the tin
plain (all-purpose) flour to dust
3 eggs, separated
50 g (2 oz/¼ cup) caster (superfine) sugar
finely grated zest of ½ unwaxed lemon
finely grated zest of ½ orange
I teaspoon baking powder
I tablespoon brandy (or water)
20 g (¾ oz/3 tablespoons) ground almonds (almond meal)
40 g (1½ oz/⅓ cup) fine semolina (semolina flour)
icing sugar to serve

SYRUP
100g (3½ oz/scant ½ cup) caster (superfine) sugar
juice of ½ lemon
thinly pared zest of ½ unwaxed lemon

Preheat the oven to 200°C (400°F/Gas 6).

Butter a 20 cm (8 in) spring-form cake tin, then dust with a little flour.

Whisk the egg whites until they form stiff peaks. Beat the yolks and sugar together until creamy and add the citrus zests. Mix the baking powder with the brandy (or water) and stir to dissolve. Add to the egg yolk mixture, then add the almonds and semolina. Beat well.

Fold in the egg whites with a metal spoon, stopping as soon as everything is mixed together, to keep as much air in the mixture as possible.

Pour the batter into the prepared tin and bake in the oven for 20 minutes.

To make the syrup bring 125 ml (4 fl oz/½ cup) of water, the sugar and lemon juice to the boil and boil for 10 minutes, reducing by about a quarter.

When the cake has cooked it will have risen slightly and be golden-brown all over. Prick the cake all over with a cocktail stick or toothpick, then evenly pour over the syrup (you may not need all of it, so pour gradually). Cover and set aside. Leave overnight for the syrup to soak into the cake.

When ready to serve, grate over a little lemon zest and dust with icing sugar.

ØLIVE ØIL CHØCØLATE MØUSSE

A decadent dessert and a great way to make chocolate mousse without raw eggs. This is very rich, so serve small portions.

Avoid using peppery or bitter olive oils, as those flavours will come through and clash with the chocolate. Rather than almonds, try pistachios crumbled on top; make it even more decadent by stirring through 2 tablespoons of brandy or orange liqueur; or liven it up by adding a shot of cold espresso.

SERVES 4

2 tablespoons flaked almonds
125 g (4 oz) dark (bittersweet) chocolate (70% cocoa solids minimum)
1 tablespoon caster (superfine) sugar, plus more if needed
3 tablespoons mild-tasting extra-virgin olive oil
120 ml (4 fl oz/½ cup) double (heavy) cream
pinch of fine salt
¼ teaspoon vanilla extract
finely grated zest of ½ orange, plus more to serve (optional)

Gently stir the flaked almonds in a dry pan over a medium heat, until lightly toasted. Set aside.

In a bain-marie or a heatproof bowl set over just simmering water, melt the chocolate and sugar together, stirring. Don't allow the bowl to touch the water or the chocolate will overheat. Once the chocolate has just melted, mix in the oil and remove from the heat.

Whip the cream until it forms soft peaks when you lift the beaters from the bowl. Allow the chocolate to cool slightly, but don't allow it to set. Stir in the salt, vanilla extract, orange zest (if using) or any other flavourings you're using now. Gently fold the chocolate mix into the whipped cream with a metal spoon, being careful not to knock the air out of the cream. Taste to check it is sweet enough and add a little more sugar if necessary.

Scoop spoonfuls of the mousse into 4 ramekins or individual serving dishes and place in the fridge to chill for 30 minutes. Sprinkle with the almonds just before serving, adding orange zest, if you included it in the mousse.

DESSERTS, SWEETS & DRINKS

Index

REBECCA SEAL is a food and drink writer. She writes for newspapers such as the *Financial Times, Observer, Evening Standard, Guardian* and the *Times*, and magazines such as *Olive* and *Grazia*, as well as making frequent appearances on Channel 4. Her previous book was *Istanbul: Recipes from the heart of Turkey*. She lives in London with her partner, photographer Steven Joyce.

rebeccaseal.co.uk

STEVEN JOYCE is a photographer specialising in food, portraiture and travel. His work regularly features in national newspapers, magazines and recipe books.

stevenjoyce.com

Acknowledgements

A huge number of people helped Steven and I put this book together, feeding us delicious food and helping us in our madcap schemes to visit as many islands as possible. In London, Sofia Panayiotaki and Alexandros Konstantinou, along with their PR team at Media Co (especially Veta Chatziioannou and Aaron Moore), went miles out of their way to make our research trips successful, as did Christina Kalogera from the Greek National Tourism Organisation UK office, and we are extremely grateful to them all.

On Crete, we'd like to thank Theano Vrentzou-Skordalaki, deputy governor of Crete, who took time to talk to us about Cretan diet and its history; everyone at Thalori, an extraordinary retreat on the mountainous south side of Crete, built from the ruins of an ancient village (thalori.com); Stelios Trilirakis and his family at Ntounias restaurant (ntounias.gr), who took us around his wonderful farm and showed us how he grows squash and apples on rocky terraces, before feeding us one of our best meals on Crete; Matsikas Spiros from Mohlakis cheese (mohlakis.com) who talked me through all of his hand-made cheeses in the covered market in Chania; Georgios Kallinterakis at Ta Bakaliarakia in Chania, who gave us salt cod to eat and a lot of raki to drink one lunchtime; Giorgios Skoulaxinos and Judy Smith from Creta Palace in Rethymnon (grecotel.com/crete/creta-palace), who generously put us up at very short notice in a blissfully pretty suite.

On Rhodes, we'd like to thank Mariza Sviriades, owner of the luxurious Lindian Village hotel (lindianvillage.gr), for treating us to wine tastings, cooking lessons with her brilliant chefs (who taught us how to make local pies and dips, as well as wobbly-centred galaktoboureko, perhaps the best named dessert in the world), and gave us the most beautiful room (with its own swimming pool!); the hotel manager who introduced us to the famous Sheep Rustler or Bandit's Retreat restaurant, Tou Limeri Tou Listi, in the mountain village of Profilia, owned by chef Savvas, who served the most delicious slow-cooked meats and meze and showed us the secrets of his wood oven (don't miss his food or the mountainous interior of Rhodes if you visit); Sofia Mailli, who took me for a day with a women's cooperative in the village of Apollonia, where we both learnt how to make traditional sweets from the lovely and very patient Katerina Palazi; the family at Perigiali at Stegna (perigiali-parathinalos.gr) for sharing their garlic fish and tiganites recipes; and Michalis Mavrikos who spent an evening talking us through and feeding us Rhodian specialities at his family's restaurant, Mavrikos, in Lindos, another must visit on the island.

On Santorini, there are so many wonderful restaurants that we can't wait to go back for more. We'd like to thank chef Vassilis Zacharakis from Nichteri restaurant (nichteri.gr); Georgia Tsara from Selene (selene.gr); Dimitris Lazarou, whose restaurant Saltsa has sadly now closed; George Grafakos, CEO of AquaVista Hotels (aquavistahotels.com) who kindly arranged for us to stay at Above Blue Suites (abovebluesuites.com) just one of their stunning hotels, which sits on just on the edge of Santorini's volcanic caldera and is gorgeous, and whose appetite for showing us Santorini's gastronomy perfectly matched ours for consuming it; and Kirini Suites and White Cave Restaurant (kirini.com) where we had perhaps the best table in the world and certainly the house: a solitary table for two watching the sun set over the volcano itself.

On Milos, we'd like to thank the mayor, Gerasimos Damoulakis, and his family, for introducing us to Virginia (Gina) Grigorious. Gina was a brilliant guide to the island and took us to Armenaki (armenaki.gr), where we learnt about traditional fish soups and local wines from owner Antonis Mavrogiannis who also arranged for Steven to photograph some local fishermen; to Sirocco (restaurantsirocco.gr) where we ate meat cooked under volcanic sand by Stella Tseroni; to Paleos in Plaka where we tried ladenia pastries and watermelon pie cooked by Vasiliki Drounga; to Paradossiaka Edesmata, a shop in Adamas with wonderful ice cream and freshly made pastas; and finally to O! Chamos, where we ate dishes cooked to Athina Psatha's family recipes until we could barely move. If you want somewhere relaxing to stay on Milos, go for Kapetan Tasos Suites (kapetantasos.gr).

On Kos, thank you to Leonidas Tsagaris, who put us up at his Santa Marina Apartments (hotelsantamarina-kos.gr) and without whom we would not have found either Mummy's Cooking or Sxoloarhio (the Old School House), where we discovered some terrific dishes to write about.

On Mykonos, we'd like to thank the team at Petinos Hotel and Blue Myth restaurant, who shared tales of the island in the 1960s, film stars and Greek dancing with tables in their teeth.

Back home, thank you to Owen Wall (owenwall.co.uk) for lending us so many of the beautiful ceramics you can see in Steven's photographs; to Tom Groves for saving the day and developing film when we needed it; and of course to Stephen King, Kate Pollard, Kajal Mistry, Emma Marijewycz and Jennifer Seymour at Hardie Grant for being a delight to work with, once again, and to Nicky Barneby for her thoughtful and elegant design. Our parents have been there to help build us up when we needed it, and our friends have been hugely supportive too, despite us being awfully antisocial for months on end.

Finally, from me, thank you to Steven Joyce. His vision, drive and ability to get up before dawn made this book what it is.

First published as *Islands of Greece* in 2014 by Hardie Grant Books
This new edition published in 2016 by Hardie Grant Books

Hardie Grant Books (UK)
5th & 6th Floors
52–54 Southwark Street
London SE1 1UN
www.hardiegrant.co.uk

Hardie Grant Books (Australia)
Ground Floor, Building 1
658 Church Street
Melbourne, VIC 3121
www.hardiegrant.com.au

British Library Cataloguing-in-Publication Data. A catalogue record
for this book is available from the British Library.

ISBN 978-1-78488-061-3

Publisher: Kate Pollard
Senior Editor: Kajal Mistry
Editorial Assistant: Hannah Roberts
Photographer © Steven Joyce
Cover and Internal Design: Nicky Barneby
Cover Illustration: Ryo Takemasa
Editor: Lucy Bannell
Proofreader: Susan Pegg
Indexer: Cathy Heath
Colour Reproduction by p2d

Printed and bound in China by 1010

10 9 8 7 6 5 4 3 2 1